DISCOURSE ON METAPHYSICS AND THE MONADOLOGY

By GOTTFRIED LEIBNIZ

Translated by
GEORGE R. MONTGOMERY

Discourse on Metaphysics and the Monadology
By Gottfried Leibniz
Translated by George R. Montgomery

Print ISBN 13: 978-1-4209-7173-6
eBook ISBN 13: 978-1-4209-7174-3

Cover Image: a detail of a portrait of Gottfried Wilhelm Leibniz, French School, (19th century) / © Look and Learn / Bridgeman Images.

Please visit *www.digireads.com*

CONTENTS

Introduction

By Paul Janet

When Descartes, in the first half of the seventeenth century, said that there are only two kinds of things or substances in nature, namely, extended substances and thinking substances, or bodies and spirits; that, in bodies, everything is reducible to extension with its modifications of form, divisibility, rest and motion, while in the soul everything is reducible to thinking with its various modes of pleasure, pain, affirmation, reasoning, will, etc. . . . ; when he in fact reduced all nature to a vast mechanism, outside of which there is nothing but the soul which manifests to itself its existence and its independence through the consciousness of its thinking, he brought about the most important revolution in modern philosophy. To understand its significance however, an account must be given of the philosophical standpoint of the time.

In all the schools at that time the dominant theory was that of the Peripatetics, altered by time and misunderstood, the theory of *substantial forms*. It posited in each kind of substance a special entity which constituted the reality and the specific difference of that substance independently of the relation of its parts. For example, according to a Peripatetic of the time, "fire differs from water not only through the position of its parts but through an entity which belongs to it quite distinct from the materials. When a body changes its condition, there is no change in the parts, but one form is supplanted by another."[1] Thus, when water becomes ice, the Peripatetics claimed that a new form substituted itself in place of the preceding form to constitute a new body. Not only did they admit primary or basal entities, or substantial forms to explain the differences in substances, but for small changes also, and for all the sensible qualities they had what were called *accidental forms*: thus hardness, heat, light were beings quite different from the bodies in which they were found.

To avoid the difficulties inherent in this theory, the Schoolmen were led to adopt infinite divisions among the substantial forms. In this way the Jesuits of Coimbre admitted three kinds of these forms: first, the being which does not receive its existence from a superior being and is not received into an inferior subject,—this being is God; second, the forces which receive their being from elsewhere without being themselves received into matter,—these are the forms which are entirely free from any corporeal concretion; third, the forms dependent

---

[1] L. P. Lagrange, *Les Principes de la Philosophie contre les Nouveaux Philosophes.*—See Bouillier's *Histoire de la Philosophie Cartesienne*, Vol. I, Chap. 26.

in every respect, which obtain their being from a superior cause and are received into a subject,—these are the accidents and the substantial forms which determine matter.

Other schoolmen adopted divisions still more minute and distinguished six classes of substantial forms, as follows: first, the forms of primary matter or of the elements; second, those of inferior compounds, like stones; third, those of higher compounds, like drugs; fourth, those of living beings, like plants; fifth, those of sensible beings, like animals; sixth, above all the rest, the reasoning (*rationalis*) substantial form which is like the others in so far as it is the form of a body but which does not derive from the body its special function of thinking.

Some have thought, perhaps, that Molière, Nicole, Malebranche and all those who in the seventeenth century ridiculed the substantial forms, calumniated the Peripatetic Schoolmen and gratuitously imputed absurdities to them. But they should read the following explanation, given by Toletus, of the production of fire: "The substantial form of fire," says Toletus, "is an active principle by which fire with heat for an instrument produces fire." Is not this explanation even more absurd than the *virtus dormitiva*? The author goes on to raise an objection, that fire does not always come from fire. To explain this he proceeds, "I reply that there is the greatest difference between the accidental and the substantial forms. The accidental forms have not only a repugnance but a definite repugnance, as between white and black, while between substantial forms there is a certain repugnance but it is not definite, because the substantial form repels equally all things. Therefore it follows that white which is an accidental form results only from white and not from black, while fire can result from all the substantial forms capable of producing it in air, in water or in any other thing."

The theory of substantial or accidental forms did more than to lead to nonsense like the above; it introduced errors which stood in the way of any clear investigation of real causes. For example, since some bodies fell toward the earth while others rose in the air, it was said that gravity was the substantial form of the former and lightness of the latter. Thus heavy and light bodies were distinguished as two classes of bodies having properties essentially different, and they were kept from the inquiry whether these apparently different phenomena did not have an identical cause and could not be explained by the same law. It was thus again that seeing water rise in an empty tube, instead of inquiring under what more general fact this phenomena could be subserved, they imagined a *virtue*, an occult *quality*, a *hatred* on the part of the vacuum, and this not only concealed the ignorance under a word void of sense but it made science impossible because a metaphor was taken for an explanation.

So great had become the abuse of the *substantial forms*, the *occult qualities*, the *sympathetic virtues*, etc., that it was a true deliverance when Gassendi on the one hand and Descartes on the other founded a new physics on the principle that there is nothing in the body which is not contained in the mere conception of bodies, namely extension. According to these new philosophers all the phenomena of bodies are only modifications of extension and should be explained by the properties inherent in extension, namely, form, position, and motion. Upon this principle nothing happens in bodies of which the understanding is not able to form a clear and distinct idea. Modern physics seems to have partially confirmed this theory, when it explains sound and light by movements (vibrations, undulations, oscillations, etc.), either of air or of ether.

It has often been said that the march of modern science has been in the opposite direction from the Cartesian philosophy, in that the latter conceives of matter as a dead and inert substance while the former represents it as animated by forces, activities and energies of every kind. This it seems to me is to confuse two wholly different points of view, that is the physical and the metaphysical points of view. The fact seems to be that from the physical point of view, science has rather followed the line of Descartes, reducing the number of occult qualities and as far as possible explaining all the phenomena in terms of motion. In this way all the problems tend to become problems of mechanics; change of position, change of form, change of motion—these are the principles to which our physicists and our chemists have recourse whenever they can.

It is therefore wrong to say that the Cartesian line of thought has completely failed and that modern science has been moving away from it more and more. On the contrary we are witnessing the daily extension of mechanicalism in the science of our time. The question takes on a different phase when it is asked whether mechanicalism is the final word of nature, whether it is self-sufficient, in fact whether the principles of mechanicalism are themselves mechanical. This is a wholly metaphysical question and does not at all affect positive science; for the phenomena will be explained in the same way whether matter is thought of as inert, composed of little particles which are moved and combined by invisible hands, or whether an interior activity and a sort of spontaneity is attributed to them. For the physicist and for the chemist, forces are only words representing unknown causes. For the metaphysician they are real activities. It is metaphysics, therefore, and not physics which is rising above mechanicalism. It is in metaphysics that mechanicalism has found, not its contradiction, but its completion through the doctrine of dynamism. It is this latter direction that philosophy has mainly taken since Descartes and in this the prime mover was Leibniz.[2]

In order to understand Leibniz's system we must not forget a point to which sufficient attention has not been paid, namely, that Leibniz never gave up or rejected the mechanicalism of Descartes. He always affirmed that everything in nature could be explained mechanically; that, in the explanation of phenomena, recourse must never be had to occult causes; so far indeed did he press this position that he refused to admit Newton's attraction of gravitation, suspecting it of being an

---

[2] We give here in a note the résumé of Leibniz's life and the names of his principal works. Leibniz (Gottfried Wilhelm) was born at Leipzig in 1646. He lost his father at the age of six years. From his very infancy he gave evidence of remarkable ability. At fifteen years of age he was admitted to the higher branches of study (philosophy and mathematics) which he pursued first at Leipzig and then at Jena. An intrigue not very well understood prevented his obtaining his doctor's degree at Leipzig and he obtained it from the small university of Altdorf near Nuremberg, where he made the acquaintance of Baron von Boineburg, who became one of his most intimate friends and who took him to Frankfort. Here he was named as a councilor of the supreme court in the electorate of Mainz, and wrote his first two works on jurisprudence, *The Study of Law* and *The Reform of the Corpus Juris*. At Frankfort also were written his first literary and philosophical works and notably his two treatises on motion: *Abstract Motion*, addressed to the Academy of Sciences at Paris, and *Concrete Motion*, addressed to the Royal Society at London. He remained with the Elector till the year 1672, when he began his journeys. He first went to Paris and then to London, where he was made a member of the Royal Society. Returning to Paris he remained till 1677, when he made a trip through Holland, and finally took up his residence at Hanover, where he was appointed director of the library. At Hanover he lived for ten years, leading a very busy life. He contributed to the founding of the *Acta Eruditorum*, a sort of journal of learning. From 1687 to 1691, at the request of his patron, Duke Ernst-Augustus, he was engaged in searching various archives in Germany and Italy for the writing of the history of the houses of Brunswick. To him the Academy of Berlin, of which he was the first president, owes its foundation. The last fifteen years of his life were given up principally to philosophy. In this period must be placed the *New Essays*, the *Theodicy*, the *Monadology*, and also his correspondence with Clarke, which was interrupted by his death—November 14, 1716. For fuller details, see Guhrauer's learned and complete biography, 2 vols., Breslau, 1846. During the life-time of Leibniz, aside from the articles in journals, only some five of his writings were published, including his doctor's thesis, *De Principio Individui* (1663), and the *Théodicée* (1710). After his death (1716) all his papers were deposited in the library at Hanover, where they are to-day, a great part of them (15,000 letters) still unpublished. In 1717–1719 appeared the Correspondence with Locke; in 1720 a German translation of the *Monadology*; in 1765 his Oeuvres Philosophiques, etc., including the New Essays on the Human Understanding; in 1768 Duten's edition of his works in six volumes; in 1840 appeared Erdmann's edition of his works, including among other unpublished writings the original French of the Monadology. *The Correspondence with Arnauld* and the *Treatise on Metaphysics* were first published by Grotefend in 1840. Gerhardt published Leibniz's mathematical works 1843 to 1863, and the *Philosophical Works* (seven volumes), 1875-1890. In 1900 Paul Janet, who had already published the *Philosophical Works* (1866) in two volumes, brought out a second edition, revised and enlarged. The first English translation of Leibniz's works was made by Professor G. M. Duncan, who included in one volume all of the better known shorter works (1890). This was followed in 1896 with a translation of the *New Essays* by A. G. Langley. Latta's translation of some of the shorter works, including the *Monadology*, has earned a well-merited reputation, and Russell's work on Leibniz's philosophy contains much that is suggestive to a translator.

occult quality: while, however, Leibniz admitted with Descartes the application of mechanicalism he differed from him in regard to the basis of it and he is continually repeating that if everything in nature is mechanical, geometrical and mathematical the source of mechanicalism is in metaphysics.[3]

Descartes explained everything geometrically and mechanically, that is by extension, form, and motion, just as Democritus had done before; but he did not go farther, finding in extension the very essence of corporeal substance. Leibniz's genius showed itself when he pointed out that extension does not suffice to explain phenomena and that it has need itself of an explanation. Brought up in the scholastic and peripatetic philosophy, he was naturally predisposed to accord more of reality to the corporeal substance, and his own reflections soon carried him much farther along the same line.

It is also worth noticing, as Guhrauer has said in his *Life of Leibniz*, that it was a theological problem which put Leibniz upon the track of reforming the conception of substance. The question was rife as to the real presence in transubstantiation. This problem seemed inexplicable upon the Cartesian hypothesis, for if the essence of a body is its extension, it is a contradiction that the same body can be found in several places at the same time. Leibniz, writing to Arnauld in 1671, says he thinks he has found the solution to this great problem since he has discovered "that the essence of a body does not consist in extension, that the corporeal substance, even taken by itself, is not extension and is not subject to the conditions of extension. This would have been evident if the real character of substance had been discovered sooner."

Leaving aside this point, however, the following are the different considerations which led Leibniz to admit non-mechanical principles as above corporeal mechanicalism, and to reduce the idea of the body to the idea of active indivisible substances, entelechies or monads, having innate within themselves the reason for all their determinations.

1. The first and principal reason which Leibniz brings up against Descartes is that, "If all that there is in bodies is extension and the position of the parts, then when two bodies come into contact and move on together after the contact, that one which was in motion will carry along the body at rest without losing any of its velocity, and the difference in the sizes of the bodies will effect no change," which is

---

[3] Letter to Schulemburg (Dutens, T. III, p. 332): "The Cartesians rightly felt that all particular phenomena of bodies are produced mechanically, but they failed to see that the sources of mechanicalism in turn arise in some other cause." Letter to Rémond de Montmort (Erdmann, *Opera Philosophica*, p. 702): "When I seek for the ultimate reasons of mechanicalism and the laws of motion I am surprised to discover that they are not to be found in mathematics and that we must turn to metaphysics."—See also: *De Natura Ipsa*, 3; *De Origine Radicali*; *Animadversiones in Cartesium*, Guhrauer, p. 80), etc.

contrary to experience. A body in motion which comes in contact with one at rest loses some of its velocity and its direction is modified, which would not happen if the body were purely passive. "Higher conceptions must therefore be added to extension, namely, the conceptions of substance, action and force; these latter carry the idea that that which suffers action, acts reciprocally and that that which acts is reacted upon."[4]

2. Extension cannot serve to give the reason for the changes which take place in bodies, for extension with its various modifications constitutes what is called in the school terminology extrinsic characteristics, whence nothing can result for the being itself; whether a body be round or square does not affect its interior condition, nor can any particular change result for it.[5] Furthermore, every philosophy which is exclusively mechanical is obliged to deny change and to hold that everything is changeless and that there are only modifications of position or displacements in space or motion. Who does not see, however, that motion itself is a change, and should have its reason in the being which moves or which is moved, for even passive motion must correspond to something in the essence of the body moved? Besides if corporeal elements differ from one another through form, why have they one form rather than any other? Epicurus talks to us of round and hooked atoms. Why is a certain atom round and another hooked? Should not the reason be in the very substance of the atom? Therefore form, position, motion and all the extrinsic modifications of bodies should emanate from an internal principle analogous to that which Aristotle calls *nature* or *entelechy*.[6]

3. Extension cannot be substance. On the contrary it presupposes substance. "Aside from extension there must be a subject which is extended, that is, a substance to which continuity appertains. For extension signifies only a continued repetition or multiplication of that which is expanded, a plurality, a continuity or co-existence of parts and consequently it does not suffice to explain the real nature of expanded or repeated substance whose conception precedes that of repetition."[7]

4. Another reason given by Leibniz is that the conception of substance necessarily implies the idea of unity. No one thinks that two

---

[4] Letter, Whether the essence of bodies consists in extension, 1691 (Erdmann, Vol. 27, p. 112).

[5] "Extension is an attribute which cannot constitute a complete being from it can be obtained neither action nor change; it expresses merely a present condition but in no case the past or future, as the conception of a substance should."—Letter to Arnauld.

[6] *Confessio Naturae Contra Artheista*, 1668, Erdm., p. 45. Leibniz in this little treatise proves: 1st, that bodies and indeed atoms have not in themselves the reason for their forms; 2d, that they have not the reason for their motion; 3d, that they have not the reason for their coherence.

[7] Extract from a letter (Erdmann, Vol. 28, p. 115): Examination of the principles of Malebranche (Erdmann, p. 692).

stones very far apart form a single substance. If now we imagine them joined and soldered together, will this juxtaposition change the nature of things? Of course not; there will always be two stones and not a single one. If now we imagine them attached by an irresistible force, the impossibility of separating them will not prevent the mind from distinguishing them and will not prevent their remaining two and not one. In a word every compound is no more a single substance than is a pile of sand or a sack of wheat. We might as well say that the employees of the India Company formed a single substance.[8] It is evident therefore that a compound is never a substance and in order to find the real substance we must attain unity or the indivisible. To say that there are no such unities is to say that matter has no elements, in other words that it is not made up of substance but it is a pure phenomenon like the rainbow. The conclusion is then either that matter has no substantial reality or else it must be admitted that it is reducible to simple and consequently unextended elements, called *monads*.

5. Leibniz brings forward another argument in behalf of his theory of monads. This is that the essence of every substance is in force, which fact is as true of the soul as of the body. It can be proved *a priori*. Is it not evident that a being really exists only in so far as it acts? A being absolutely passive would be a pure nothing, and would involve a contradiction; or, by hypothesis, receiving everything from outside and having nothing through itself, it would have no characteristic, no attribute and hence would be a pure nothing. The mere fact of existence, therefore, already supposes a certain force and a certain energy.

Leibniz presses this thought of the activity of substances so far that he even admits no degree of passivity. According to him, no substance is, properly speaking, passive. Passion in a substance is nothing else than an action considered bound to another action in another substance. Every substance acts only through itself and cannot act upon any other. The monads have no windows through which to receive anything from outside. They do not undergo any action and consequently are never passive. All that takes place in them is the spontaneous development of their own essence. All that there is, is that the states of each one

---

[8] "If the parts which act together for a common purpose, more properly compose a substance than do those which are in contact, then all the officials of the India Company would much better constitute a real substance than would a pile of stones. What else, however, is a common purpose rather than a resemblance or indeed an orderliness which our minds notice in different things? If on the other hand the unity by contact be made the basis, other difficulties arise. The parts of solid bodies are united perhaps only by the pressure of surrounding bodies, while in themselves and in their substance there is no more union than in a heap of sand (*arena sine calce*). Why do many rings when interlaced to form a chain compose a veritable substance rather than when there are openings so that they can be taken apart? . . . They are all fictions of the mind." (Letter to Arnauld).

correspond to the states of all the others. When we consider one of these states in one monad as corresponding to a certain other state in another monad, in such a way that the latter is the condition of the former, the first state is called a *passion* and the second an *action*. There is, therefore, between all monad-substances a pre-established harmony, in accordance with which each one represents (or expresses, as Leibniz says) the whole universe. But this is ever only the development of its own activity.

In restoring to created substances the activity which the Cartesian school had too much sacrificed, Leibniz thought to contribute to the clearer distinction between the created and the Creator. He justly remarked that the more the activity of the created things is diminished, the more necessary becomes the intervention of God, in such a way that if all activity in created things is suppressed, then we must say that it is God who brings everything in them to pass and who is at the same time their being and their action (*operari et esse*). What difference, however, is there between this point of view and that of Spinoza? Would we not thus make nature the life and the development of the divine nature? In fact, by this hypothesis, nature is reduced to a mass of modes of which God is the substance. He, therefore, is all that there is of reality in bodies as well as in spirits.

To these five fundamental reasons given by Leibniz it will perhaps be allowed us to add a few particular considerations.

Those who deny that the essence of bodies is only in force, either admit the vacuum with the atomists, ancient and modern, or else like the Cartesians they do not admit it. Let us take up each of these positions separately.

For the atomists, disciples of Democritus and of Epicurus, or of Gassendi, the universe is composed of two elements, the vacuum and the plenum, on the one hand space and on the other hand bodies. The bodies are reducible to a certain number of solid corpuscles, indivisible, with differing forms, heavy and animated by an essential and spontaneous motion. These are the atoms which by their coming together constitute bodies.

Now it is evident that atoms in taking the place of other atoms, successively occupy in empty space places that are adequate to them, which have exactly the same extension and the same forms as the respective atoms. If at the moment when an atom is motionless in some place we imagine lines drawn following its contours (as when an object is being traced for transferring), is it not clear that if the atom were removed, we should have preserved its effigy, or a sort of silhouette, its geometric form upon a foundation of empty space? We should obtain thus a portion of space, which I will call an empty atom, in contrast with the full atom which was there before.

Now I ask the atomists to explain what distinguishes the full atom from the empty one, what are the characteristics that may be found in one and not in the other. Is it the being extended? No, for the empty atom is extended like the full atom. Is it the having a form? No, for the empty atom has a form as has the full atom and exactly the same form. Is it the being indivisible? No, for it is still more difficult to understand the divisibility of space than of the body. In a word everything which depends on extension is the same in the empty atom as in the full atom. But the empty atom is not a body and contains nothing corporeal; therefore extension is not the essence of bodies and perhaps does not constitute a part of this essence. May we say that it is the motion which distinguishes the full atom from the empty atom? But before beginning to move the atom must have already been something, because that which is nothing in itself can be neither at rest, nor in motion. Motion, therefore, is a dependent and subordinate phenomenon which already presupposes a defined essence. If we examine carefully we will see that what really distinguishes the full atom from the empty atom is its solidity or weight. Neither solidity nor weight, however, are modifications of extension; both come from force. It is accordingly, force and not extension which constitutes the essence of the body.

Turning now to those who, like the Cartesians, are unwilling to admit the possibility of a vacuum and maintain that all space is full, the demonstration is still more simple, for we may ask in what filled space, taken in its entirety, differs from empty space taken in its entirety. Both are infinite; both are ideally divisible and both are really indivisible; both are susceptible of modalities in form or of geometrically defined forms. Perhaps it will be claimed that in full space the particles are movable and can supplant one another; in this case we are back in the preceding line of argument and we shall ask in what these movable particles are distinguished from the immovable particles of space among which they move. Thus the Cartesians, like the atomists, will be obliged to recognize that the plenum is distinguished from the vacuum only by resistance, solidity, motion, activity, in a word, force.

To those who reproach the Leibnizian conception with idealizing matter too much, it may be replied that matter taken in itself is necessarily ideal and super-sensible. Of course it cannot be said that a body is only an assembly of subjective modifications. The Berkeleyan idealism is a superficial idealism, which will not stand examination; for when I shall have reduced the whole universe to a dream of my mind and to an expansion of myself the question will still remain whence comes this my dream and what are the causes which have produced in me so complicated a hallucination; these causes are outside of me and they go beyond me on every side; it would therefore be very inappropriate for me to call them *myself*, for the I is strictly that of which I have consciousness. The Fichtean *Ich*, which by reaction against itself thus produces the *nicht-ich* is only a complicated and artificial circumlocution for saying in a paradoxical form that there is a not-I. At most, we can conjecture with the absolute idealism that the I and the not-I are only two faces of one and the same being, which involves them both in an infinite activity; but we thus reach a position very far from the idealism of Berkeley.

To return to the idealism of Leibniz, I think it can be shown *a priori* that matter taken in itself is something ideal and super-sensible, at least to those who admit a divine intelligence. For it will readily be granted that God does not know matter by means of the senses; for it is an axiom in metaphysics that God has no senses and consequently cannot have sensations. Thus: God can be neither warm nor cold; he cannot smell the odor of flowers; he cannot hear sounds, he cannot see colors; he cannot feel electrical disturbances, etc. In a word, since he is a pure intelligence he can conceive only the purely intelligible; not that he is ignorant of any of the phenomena of nature, only that he knows them in their intelligible reasons and not through their sensible impressions, by means of which creatures are aware of them. Sensibility supposes a subject with senses, organs and nerves, that is, it is a relation between created things. From God's point of view, therefore, matter is not sensible; it is, as the Germans say, *übersinnlich*. The conclusion is easy to draw, namely, that God, being absolute intelligence, necessarily sees things as they are, and conversely the things in themselves are such as he sees them. Matter is, accordingly, such in itself as God sees it, but he sees it only in its ideal and intelligible essence; whence we see that matter is an intelligible something and not something sensible.

To be sure we may not conclude from this point that the essence of matter does not consist in extension, for it could be maintained that extension is an object of pure intelligence quite as well as force. But without taking up the difficulty of disengaging extension from every sensible element, I wish to establish only one thing, namely that Leibniz cannot be reproached with idealizing matter, since this must be done in every system, at least in those which admit a divine *logos* and a foreordaining reason.

One of the most widely spread objections against the monadological system is the impossibility of composing an extended whole out of non-extended elements. This is Euler's principal objection in one of his Letters to a German Princess and he considered it absolutely definitive because the necessary consequence of such a system would be to deny the reality of extension and of space, and to launch out thus into all the difficulties of the idealistic labyrinth. I think, however, that Euler's objection is not at all insoluble, and that it is even possible to separate the system of monads from the system of the ideality of space. It can be shown that all the questions relating to space can be adjourned or kept back without compromising the hypothesis of the monads.

For, let us suppose with the atomists, with Clarke and Newton the reality of space, vacuums, and atoms. It is no more difficult to conceive of monads in space than of atoms; a point of indivisible activity might be at a certain point of space and a collection of the points of activity would constitute the mass which we call a body. Now, even if we grant that these points of activity are separated by space, yet when they were taken together they might produce upon the senses the impression of continuous space. Even in the case of what is called a body, say a marble table, every one knows that there are forces, that is to say, vacuums, between the parts. Since these vacuums, however, escape our sense organs, the body appears to us to be continuous, like the circle described by a moving succession of luminous points. In fact the bodies would be composed, as the Pythagoreans have already said, of two elements; the intervals (διαστήματα) and the monads (μόναδες); except that the Pythagorean monads were mere geometric points, while for Leibniz they are active points, radiating centers of activity, energies.

Regarding the difficulty of admitting into space forces non-extended and consequently having no relation to space, I grant that it is very serious. It cannot be raised, however, by those who consider the soul as a non-extended force and as an individual substance; for they are obliged to recognize that it is in space although in its essence it has no relation to space; there is, therefore, for them no contradiction in holding that a simple force is in space. If, on the other hand, it be denied that the soul is in space, that it is in the body, and even that it is in a certain part of the body, is it not clear that this would be attributing to the soul a character which is true only of God? To be sure, those who consider the soul as a divine idea, an eternal form temporarily united to an individual, might speak thus. Thus regarded, with the idealists or with Spinoza, the soul is not in space. But if the soul is represented as an individual and created substance, how can it be thought of except as in space and in the body to which it is united? Still more, therefore, in the case of monads will we be obliged to admit that they may be in space and then, as we have seen, the appearance of extension is explained without difficulty.

If, now, instead of admitting the reality of space we hold with Leibniz or with Kant that it is ideal, the system of monads offers no longer any serious difficulty, except from the point of view of those who deny the plurality of individual substances. In any case Euler's objection evidently loses its force.

Another difficulty raised against the monadology is that it effaces the distinction between the soul and the body. This difficulty seems to me like the preceding one to be merely apparent. Because in every hypothesis, the essential distinction between the body and the soul is that the body is a composite, while the soul is simple. In order to prove that the soul is not extended the proof is offered that it is not a composite, while the body on the contrary is. Now in Leibniz's hypothesis also, the body is only a composite, only an aggregation of simple elements. What difference does the nature of the elements make in this case? It is the whole, it is the aggregation which we contrast with the soul; and in Leibniz's hypothesis, quite as well as in that of Descartes, the body as an aggregation is wholly incapable of thought.

Some one will reply: "granting all that, the elements are nevertheless single and indivisible like the soul itself and they are therefore of the same nature as the soul—they are souls themselves." This last consequence is very incorrectly drawn, however.

What is meant by the words: "of the same nature"? Does it mean that the monads which compose the body are feeling, thinking, willing beings? Leibniz never said such a thing. What is the basis for affirming that the particles of my body are thinking substances? Let us look at the semblance they have to the soul. Doubtless they are like it single and indivisible substances. But what difficulty does it introduce to admit that the soul and body have common attributes? The atoms, for instance, have they not in common with the soul, existence, indestructibility, self-identity? And does the argument of the identity of the ego in contrast with the changing nature of organized matter, cease to be valid, because the atom is quite as self-identical as the soul? Indeed the indestructibility of the atom is used as an analogy to establish the indestructibility of the soul. If this common character does not prevent their being distinguished, why should their being distinguished be more difficult when they have in common a character essential to all substance, namely, the attribute of activity?

Furthermore, if the atoms of the substance, which constitutes the universe, are indivisible units, the power of thinking is not inconsistent with their conception. They may be thinking substances, and it cannot be denied that in this system a monad may become, if God wishes it, a thinking soul. If on the one hand it is not impossible, there is no way, on the other hand, of proving that it may be so. Why may there not be several orders of monads which are unable to pass from one class to another? Why may there not be monads having merely mechanical properties; others of a higher order, containing the principle of life, like plant souls; still higher sensitive souls; and finally free and intelligent souls endowed with personality and immortality? Leibniz's system is no more opposed than any other to these orders.

If, however, by a bolder hypothesis, the possibility of a monad's passing from one order to another be admitted, there would still be nothing here degrading to the true dignity of man, for, after all it must be recognized that the human soul in its first state is hardly anything more than a plant-soul which lifts itself by degrees to the condition of a thinking soul. Therefore there will be no contradiction in admitting that every monad contains potentially a thinking soul. Should such a hypothesis be repugnant, I still maintain that the monadological system does not force one to it, since monadism quite as well as the popular atomism can admit a scale of substances essentially distinct from one another.

Another objection which the Leibnizian excites, and one which Arnauld does not fail to raise in one of his letters, is that the system of monads weakens the argument of a first mover, since it implies that matter can be endowed with active force and consequently with spontaneous motion. Leibniz does not meet this objection in a convincing manner and says merely that recourse must be had to God to explain the co-ordination of movements. This, however, avoids the point, for the co-ordination has no relation to the argument of the first mover, only to that of the ordering and of the arrangement which is a wholly different matter. We may, however, remark that Leibniz, in order to establish the reality of the force in corporeal substance, much more frequently uses the fact of resistance to motion, than that of the so-called spontaneous motion. For instance, one of his principal arguments is that a moving body, when it comes in contact with another, loses motion in proportion to the resistance which the other opposes to it, and this is what he calls inertia. It is evident, therefore that if a substance in repose reveals itself by its resistance to motion, the argument of the first mover, far from being weakened is, on the contrary, strengthened.

Besides this, even if a spontaneous disposition to movement, be admitted in the elements of bodies, yet experience compels us to recognize that this disposition passes over into action only upon the excitation of an exterior action because we never see a body put in motion except in the presence of another. The actual indifference to movement and to repose, which at the present time is called, in mechanics, inertia, must always be admitted, whether we posit in the body a virtual disposition to movement or whether, on the contrary, the body be considered as absolutely passive; in either case there must be a cause determining the motion; it is not necessary that this first cause produce everything in the body moved, and that it should be in some sort the total cause of the motion; sufficient is it for it to be the complementary cause as the Schoolmen used to say.

Furthermore inertia must not be confounded with absolute inactivity. Leibniz showed admirably that an absolutely passive substance would be a pure nothing; that a being is active in proportion as it is in existence; in a word, that to be and to act are one and the same thing. From the fact, however, that a substance is essentially active, it does not necessarily follow that it is endowed with spontaneous motion, for the latter is only a special mode of activity and is not the only one. For example, resistance, or impenetrability, is a certain kind of activity, but is not motion. They are mistaken, therefore, who think that the theory of active matter does away with a first cause for motion, because even if motion be essential to matter, we will still have to explain why no portion of matter is ever spontaneously in motion.

In short, according to Leibniz, every being is essentially active. That which does not act does not exist; *quid non agit non existit.* Now, whatever acts is force; therefore, everything is force or a compound of forces. The essence of matter is not, as Descartes thought, inert extension, it is action, effort, energy. Furthermore the body is a compound and the compound presupposes a simple. The forces, therefore, which compose the body are simple elements, unextended— incorporeal atoms. Thus the universe is a vast dynamism, a wise system of individual forces, harmoniously related under the direction of a primordial force, whose absolute activity permits the existence outside of itself of the appropriate activities of created things, which it directs without absorbing them. This system, therefore, may be reduced to three principal points: (1) it makes the idea of force predominate over the idea of substance, or rather reduces substance to force; (2) it sees in extension only a mode of appearance of force and compares the bodies of simple and unextended elements as more or less analogous, except in their degree, to what is called the soul; (3) it sees in the forces not only general agents or modes of action of a universal agent, as have the scientists, but it sees also individual principles, both substances and causes which are inseparable from the material, or rather which constitute matter itself; Dynamism thus understood, is only universal spiritualism.

In this introduction I have examined the different difficulties which might be raised against the Leibnizian Monadology from the point of view of the Cartesian spiritualism. They have still to be examined from the point of view of those who deny the plurality of substances, that is, from the Spinozistic or pantheistic point of view. Here, however, come in a wholly different class of ideas, which we cannot enter upon without extending this introduction beyond measure. We will merely say that the force of Leibniz's system is in the fact of individuality, of which the advocates of the unity of substance have never been able to give an explanation. It is true, we must pass here from the objective to the subjective standpoint, because it is in the consciousness that the individuality manifests itself in the most striking manner, while in nature it is more veiled. One's position, therefore, should be taken in the region of the individual consciousness in order to combat Spinozism. This point of view has been particularly developed in our day by Maine de Biran and by his school. We have been content to mention it merely, not desiring to skim over a problem which is connected with the knottiest points of metaphysics and of the philosophy of religion.

Metaphysics

I. Concerning the divine perfection and that God does everything in the
most desirable way.

The conception of God which is the most common and the most
full of meaning is expressed well enough in the words: God is an
absolutely perfect being. The implications, however, of these words fail
to receive sufficient consideration. For instance, there are many
different kinds of perfection, all of which God possesses, and each one
of them pertains to him in the highest degree.

We must also know what perfection is. One thing which can surely
be affirmed about it is that those forms or natures which are not
susceptible of it to the highest degree, say the nature of numbers or of
figures, do not permit of perfection. This is because the number which
is the greatest of all (that is, the sum of all the numbers), and likewise
the greatest of all figures, imply contradictions. The greatest
knowledge, however, and omnipotence contain no impossibility.
Consequently power and knowledge do admit of perfection, and in so
far as they pertain to God they have no limits.

Whence it follows that God who possesses supreme and infinite
wisdom acts in the most perfect manner not only metaphysically, but
also from the moral standpoint. And with respect to our selves it can be
said that the more we are enlightened and informed in regard to the
works of God the more will we be disposed to find them excellent and
conforming entirely to that which we might desire.

II. Against those who hold that there is in the works of God no
goodness, or that the principles of goodness and beauty are
arbitrary.

Therefore I am far removed from the opinion of those who
maintain that there are no principles of goodness or perfection in the
nature of things, or in the ideas which God has about them, and who
say that the works of God are good only through the formal reason that
God has made them. If this position were true, God, knowing that he is
the author of things, would not have to regard them afterwards and find
them good, as the Holy Scripture witnesses. Such anthropological
expressions are used only to let us know that excellence is recognized
in regarding the works themselves, even if we do not consider their
evident dependence on their author. This is confirmed by the fact that it
is in reflecting upon the works that we are able to discover the one who
wrought. They must therefore bear in themselves his character. I

confess that the contrary opinion seems to me extremely dangerous and closely approaches that of recent innovators who hold that the beauty of the universe and the goodness which we attribute to the works of God are chimeras of human beings who think of God in human terms. In saying, therefore, that things are not good according to any standard of goodness, but simply by the will of God, it seems to me that one destroys, without realizing it, all the love of God and all his glory; for why praise him for what he has done, if he would be equally praiseworthy in doing the contrary? Where will be his justice and his wisdom if he has only a certain despotic power, if arbitrary will takes the place of reasonableness, and if in accord with the definition of tyrants, justice consists in that which is pleasing to the most powerful? Besides it seems that every act of willing supposes some reason for the willing and this reason, of course, must precede the act. This is why, accordingly, I find so strange those expressions of certain philosophers who say that the eternal truths of metaphysics and Geometry, and consequently the principles of goodness, of justice, and of perfection, are effects only of the will of God. To me it seems that all these follow from his understanding, which does not depend upon his will any more than does his essence.

III. Against those who think that God might have made things better than he has.

No more am I able to approve of the opinion of certain modern writers who boldly maintain that that which God has made is not perfect in the highest degree, and that he might have done better. It seems to me that the consequences of such an opinion are wholly inconsistent with the glory of God. *Uti minus malum habet rationem boni, ita minus bonum habet rationem mali.* I think that one acts imperfectly if he acts with less perfection than he is capable of. To show that an architect could have done better is to find fault with his work. Furthermore this opinion is contrary to the Holy Scriptures when they assure us of the goodness of God's work. For if comparative perfection were sufficient, then in whatever way God had accomplished his work, since there is an infinitude of possible imperfections, it would always have been good in comparison with the less perfect; but a thing is little praiseworthy when it can be praised only in this way.

I believe that a great many passages from the divine writings and from the holy fathers will be found favoring my position, while hardly any will be found in favor of that of these modern thinkers. Their opinion is, in my judgment, unknown to the writers of antiquity and is a deduction based upon the too slight acquaintance which we have with the general harmony of the universe and with the hidden reasons for God's conduct. In our ignorance, therefore, we are tempted to decide audaciously that many things might have been done better.

These modern thinkers insist upon certain hardly tenable subtleties, for they imagine that nothing is so perfect that there might not have been something more perfect. This is an error. They think, indeed, that they are thus safeguarding the liberty of God. As if it were not the highest liberty to act in perfection according to the sovereign reason. For to think that God acts in anything without having any reason for his willing, even if we overlook the fact that such action seems impossible, is an opinion which conforms little to God's glory. For example, let us suppose that God chooses between A and B, and that he takes A without any reason for preferring it to B. I say that this action on the part of God is at least not praiseworthy, for all praise ought to be founded upon reason which *ex hypothesi* is not present here. My opinion is that God does nothing for which he does not deserve to be glorified.

IV. That love for God demands on our part complete satisfaction with and acquiescence in that which he has done.

The general knowledge of this great truth that God acts always in the most perfect and most desirable manner possible, is in my opinion the basis of the love which we owe to God in all things; for he who loves seeks his satisfaction in the felicity or perfection of the object loved and in the perfection of his actions. *Idem velle et idem nolle vera amicitia est.* I believe that it is difficult to love God truly when one, having the power to change his disposition, is not disposed to wish for that which God desires. In fact those who are not satisfied with what God does seem to me like dissatisfied subjects whose attitude is not very different from that of rebels. I hold therefore, that on these principles, to act conformably to the love of God it is not sufficient to force oneself to be patient, we must be really satisfied with all that comes to us according to his will. I mean this acquiescence in regard to the past; for as regards the future one should not be a quietist with the arms folded, open to ridicule, awaiting that which God will do; according to the sophism which the ancients called λόγον ἄεργον, the lazy reason. It is necessary to act conformably to the presumptive will of God as far as we are able to judge of it, trying with all our might to contribute to the general welfare and particularly to the ornamentation and the perfection of that which touches us, or of that which is nigh and so to speak at our hand. For if the future shall perhaps show that God has not wished our good intention to have its way, it does not follow that he has not wished us to act as we have; on the contrary, since he is the best of all masters, he ever demands only the right intentions, and it is for him to know the hour and the proper place to let good designs succeed.

V. In what the principles of the divine perfection consist, and that the
simplicity of the means counterbalances the richness of the effects.

It is sufficient therefore to have this confidence in God, that he has
done everything for the best and that nothing will be able to injure
those who love him. To know in particular, however, the reasons which
have moved him to choose this order of the universe, to permit sin, to
dispense his salutary grace in a certain manner,—this passes the
capacity of a finite mind, above all when such a mind has not come into
the joy of the vision of God. Yet it is possible to make some general
remarks touching the course of providence in the government of things.
One is able to say, therefore, that he who acts perfectly is like an
excellent Geometer who knows how to find the best construction for a
problem; like a good architect who utilizes his location and the funds
destined for the building in the most advantageous manner, leaving
nothing which shocks or which does not display that beauty of which it
is capable; like a good householder who employs his property in such a
way that there shall be nothing uncultivated or sterile; like a clever
machinist who makes his production in the least difficult way possible;
and like an intelligent author who encloses the most of reality in the
least possible compass.

Of all beings those which are the most perfect and occupy the least
possible space, that is to say those which interfere with one another the
least, are the spirits whose perfections are the virtues. That is why we
may not doubt that the felicity of the spirits is the principal aim of God
and that he puts this purpose into execution, as far as the general
harmony will permit. We will recur to this subject again.

When the simplicity of God's way is spoken of, reference is
specially made to the means which he employs, and on the other hand
when the variety, richness and abundance are referred to, the ends or
effects are had in mind. Thus one ought to be proportioned to the other,
just as the cost of a building should balance the beauty and grandeur
which is expected. It is true that nothing costs God anything, just as
there is no cost for a philosopher who makes hypotheses in constructing
his imaginary world, because God has only to make decrees in order
that a real world come into being; but in matters of wisdom the decrees
or hypotheses meet the expenditure in proportion as they are more
independent of one another. The reason wishes to avoid multiplicity in
hypotheses or principles very much as the simplest system is preferred
in Astronomy.

VI. That God does nothing which is not orderly, and that it is not even possible to conceive of events which are not regular.

The activities or the acts of will of God are commonly divided into ordinary and extraordinary. But it is well to bear in mind that God does nothing out of order. Therefore, that which passes for extraordinary is so only with regard to a particular order established among the created things, for as regards the universal order, everything conforms to it. This is so true that not only does nothing occur in this world which is absolutely irregular, but it is even impossible to conceive of such an occurrence. Because, let us suppose for example that some one jots down a quantity of points upon a sheet of paper helter skelter, as do those who exercise the ridiculous art of Geomancy; now I say that it is possible to find a geometrical line whose concept shall be uniform and constant, that is, in accordance with a certain formula, and which line at the same time shall pass through all of those points, and in the same order in which the hand jotted them down; also if a continuous line be traced, which is now straight, now circular, and now of any other description, it is possible to find a mental equivalent, a formula or an equation common to all the points of this line by virtue of which formula the changes in the direction of the line must occur. There is no instance of a face whose contour does not form part of a geometric line and which can not be traced entire by a certain mathematical motion. But when the formula is very complex, that which conforms to it passes for irregular. Thus we may say that in whatever manner God might have created the world, it would always have been regular and in a certain order. God, however, has chosen the most perfect, that is to say the one which is at the same time the simplest in hypotheses and the richest in phenomena, as might be the case with a geometric line, whose construction was easy, but whose properties and effects were extremely remarkable and of great significance. I use these comparisons to picture a certain imperfect resemblance to the divine wisdom, and to point out that which may at least raise our minds to conceive in some sort what cannot otherwise be expressed. I do not pretend at all to explain thus the great mystery upon which depends the whole universe.

VII. That miracles conform to the regular order although they go against the subordinate regulations; concerning that which God desires or permits and concerning general and particular intentions.

Now since nothing is done which is not orderly, we may say that miracles are quite within the order of natural operations. We use the term natural of these operations because they conform to certain subordinate regulations which we call the nature of things. For it can be said that this nature is only a custom of God's which he can change on the occasion of a stronger reason than that which moved him to use these regulations. As regards general and particular intentions, according to the way in which we understand the matter, it may be said on the one hand that everything is in accordance with his most general intention, or that which best conforms to the most perfect order he has chosen; on the other hand, however, it is also possible to say that he has particular intentions which are exceptions to the subordinate regulations above mentioned. Of God's laws, however, the most universal, i.e., that which rules the whole course of the universe, is without exceptions.

It is possible to say that God desires everything which is an object of his particular intention. When we consider the objects of his general intentions, however, such as are the modes of activities of created things and especially of the reasoning creatures with whom God wishes to co-operate, we must make a distinction; for if the action is good in itself, we may say that God wishes it and at times commands it, even though it does not take place; but if it is bad in itself and becomes good only by accident through the course of events and especially after chastisement and satisfaction have corrected its malignity and rewarded the ill with interest in such a way that more perfection results in the whole train of circumstances than would have come if that ill had not occurred,—if all this takes place we must say that God permits the evil, and not that he desired it, although he has cooperated by means of the laws of nature which he has established. He knows how to produce the greatest good from them.

VIII. In order to distinguish between the activities of God and the activities of created things we must explain the conception of an individual substance.

It is quite difficult to distinguish God's actions from those of his creatures. Some think that God does everything; others imagine that he only conserves the force that he has given to created things. How far can we say either of these opinions is right?

In the first place since activity and passivity pertain properly to individual substances (*actiones sunt suppositorum*) it will be necessary to explain what such a substance is. It is indeed true that when several predicates are attributes of a single subject and this subject is not an attribute of another, we speak of it as an individual substance, but this is not enough, and such an explanation is merely nominal. We must therefore inquire what it is to be an attribute in reality of a certain subject. Now it is evident that every true predication has some basis in the nature of things, and even when a proposition is not identical, that is, when the predicate is not expressly contained in the subject, it is still necessary that it be virtually contained in it, and this is what the philosophers call *in-esse*, saying thereby that the predicate is in the subject. Thus the content of the subject must always include that of the predicate in such a way that if one understands perfectly the concept of the subject, he will know that the predicate appertains to it also. This being so, we are able to say that this is the nature of an individual substance or of a complete being, namely, to afford a conception so complete that the concept shall be sufficient for the understanding of it and for the deduction of all the predicates of which the substance is or may become the subject. Thus the quality of king, which belonged to Alexander the Great, an abstraction from the subject, is not sufficiently determined to constitute an individual, and does not contain the other qualities of the same subject, nor everything which the idea of this prince includes. God, however, seeing the individual concept, or hæcceity, of Alexander, sees there at the same time the basis and the reason of all the predicates which can be truly uttered regarding him; for instance that he will conquer Darius and Porus, even to the point of knowing *a priori* (and not by experience) whether he died a natural death or by poison,—facts which we can learn only through history. When we carefully consider the connection of things we see also the possibility of saying that there was always in the soul of Alexander marks of all that had happened to him and evidences of all that would happen to him and traces even of everything which occurs in the universe, although God alone could recognize them all.

IX. That every individual substance expresses the whole universe in its own manner and that in its full concept is included all its experiences together with all the attendant circumstances and the whole sequence of exterior events.

There follow from these considerations several noticeable paradoxes; among others that it is not true that two substances may be exactly alike and differ only numerically, *solo numero*, and that what St. Thomas says on this point regarding angels and intelligences (*quod ibi omne individuum sit species infima*) is true of all substances, provided that the specific difference is understood as Geometers understand it in the case of figures; again that a substance will be able to commence only through creation and perish only through annihilation; that a substance cannot be divided into two nor can one be made out of two, and that thus the number of substances neither augments nor diminishes through natural means, although they are frequently transformed. Furthermore every substance is like an entire world and like a mirror of God, or indeed of the whole world which it portrays, each one in its own fashion; almost as the same city is variously represented according to the various situations of him who is regarding it. Thus the universe is multiplied in some sort as many times as there are substances, and the glory of God is multiplied in the same way by as many wholly different representations of his works. It can indeed be said that every substance bears in some sort the character of God's infinite wisdom and omnipotence, and imitates him as much as it is able to; for it expresses, although confusedly, all that happens in the universe, past, present and future, deriving thus a certain resemblance to an infinite perception or power of knowing. And since all other substances express this particular substance and accommodate themselves to it, we can say that it exerts its power upon all the others in imitation of the omnipotence of the creator.

X. That the belief in substantial forms has a certain basis in fact, but that these forms effect no changes in the phenomena and must not be employed for the explanation of particular events.

It seems that the ancients, able men, who were accustomed to profound meditations and taught theology and philosophy for several centuries and some of whom recommend themselves to us on account of their piety, had some knowledge of that which we have just said and this is why they introduced and maintained the substantial forms so much decried to-day. But they were not so far from the truth nor so open to ridicule as the common run of our new philosophers imagine. I grant that the consideration of these forms is of no service in the details of physics and ought not to be employed in the explanation of particular phenomcna. In regard to this last point, the Schoolmen were at fault, as were also the physicians of times past who followed their example, thinking they had given the reason for the properties of a body in mentioning the forms and qualities without going to the trouble of examining the manner of operation; as if one should be content to say that a clock had a certain amount of clockness derived from its form, and should not inquire in what that clockness consisted. This is indeed enough for the man who buys it, provided he surrenders the care of it to someone else. The fact, however, that there was this misunderstanding and misuse of the substantial forms should not bring us to throw away something whose recognition is so necessary in metaphysics. Since without these we will not be able, I hold, to know the ultimate principles nor to lift our minds to the knowledge of the incorporeal natures and of the marvels of God. Yet as the geometer does not need to encumber his mind with the famous puzzle of the composition of the continuum, and as no moralist, and still less a jurist or a statesman has need to trouble himself with the great difficulties which arise in conciliating free will with the providential activity of God, (since the geometer is able to make all his demonstrations and the statesman can complete all his deliberations without entering into these discussions which are so necessary and important in Philosophy and Theology), so in the same way the physicist can explain his experiments, now using simpler experiments already made, now employing geometrical and mechanical demonstrations without any need of the general considerations which belong to another sphere, and if he employs the co-operation of God, or perhaps of some soul or animating force, or something else of a similar nature, he goes out of his path quite as much as that man who, when facing an important practical question would wish to enter into profound argumentations regarding the nature of destiny and of our liberty; a fault which men quite frequently commit without realizing it when they cumber their minds with considerations regarding fate, and thus they are even sometimes turned from a good resolution or from some necessary provision.

XI. That the opinions of the theologians and of the so-called scholastic philosophers are not to be wholly despised.

I know that I am advancing a great paradox in pretending to resuscitate in some sort the ancient philosophy, and to recall *postliminio* the substantial forms almost banished from our modern thought. But perhaps I will not be condemned lightly when it is known that I have long meditated over the modern philosophy and that I have devoted much time to experiments in physics and to the demonstrations of geometry and that I, too, for a long time was persuaded of the baselessness of those "beings" which, however, I was finally obliged to take up again in spite of myself and as though by force. The many investigations which I carried on compelled me to recognize that our moderns do not do sufficient justice to Saint Thomas and to the other great men of that period and that there is in the theories of the scholastic philosophers and theologians far more solidity than is imagined, provided that these theories are employed *à propos* and in their place. I am persuaded that if some careful and meditative mind were to take the trouble to clarify and direct their thoughts in the manner of analytic geometers, he would find a great treasure of very important truths, wholly demonstrable.

XII. That the conception of the extension of a body is in a way imaginary and does not constitute the substance of the body.

But to resume the thread of our discussion, I believe that he who will meditate upon the nature of substance, as I have explained it above, will find that the whole nature of bodies is not exhausted in their extension, that is to say, in their size, figure and motion, but that we must recognize something which corresponds to soul, something which is commonly called substantial form, although these forms effect no change in the phenomena, any more than do the souls of beasts, that is if they have souls. It is even possible to demonstrate that the ideas of size, figure and motion are not so distinctive as is imagined, and that they stand for something imaginary relative to our perceptions as do, although to a greater extent, the ideas of color, heat, and the other similar qualities in regard to which we may doubt whether they are actually to be found in the nature of the things outside of us. This is why these latter qualities are unable to constitute "substance" and if there is no other principle of identity in bodies than that which has just been referred to a body would not subsist more than for a moment.

The souls and the substance-forms of other bodies are entirely different from intelligent souls which alone know their actions, and not only do not perish through natural means but indeed always retain the knowledge of what they are; a fact which makes them alone open to chastisement or recompense, and makes them citizens of the republic of the universe whose monarch is God. Hence it follows that all the other creatures should serve them, a point which we shall discuss more amply later.

XIII. As the individual concept of each person includes once for all everything which can ever happen to him, in it can be seen, *a priori* the evidences or the reasons for the reality of each event, and why one happened sooner than the other. But these events, however certain, are nevertheless contingent, being based on the free choice of God and of his creatures. It is true that their choices always have their reasons, but they incline to the choices under no compulsion of necessity.

But before going further it is necessary to meet a difficulty which may arise regarding the principles which we have set forth in the preceding. We have said that the concept of an individual substance includes once for all everything which can ever happen to it and that in considering this concept one will be able to see everything which can truly be said concerning the individual, just as we are able to see in the nature of a circle all the properties which can be derived from it. But does it not seem that in this way the difference between contingent and necessary truths will be destroyed, that there will be no place for human liberty, and that an absolute fatality will rule as well over all our actions as over all the rest of the events of the world? To this I reply that a distinction must be made between that which is certain and that which is necessary. Every one grants that future contingencies are assured since God foresees them, but we do not say just because of that that they are necessary. But it will be objected, that if any conclusion can be deduced infallibly from some definition or concept, it is necessary; and now since we have maintained that everything which is to happen to anyone is already virtually included in his nature or concept, as all the properties are contained in the definition of a circle, therefore, the difficulty still remains. In order to meet the objection completely, I say that the connection or sequence is of two kinds; the one, absolutely necessary, whose contrary implies contradiction, occurs in the eternal verities like the truths of geometry; the other is necessary only *ex hypothesi*, and so to speak by accident, and in itself it is contingent since the contrary is not implied. This latter sequence is not founded upon ideas wholly pure and upon the pure understanding of God, but upon his free decrees and upon the processes of the universe. Let us give an example. Since Julius Caesar will become perpetual Dictator and master of the Republic and will overthrow the liberty of Rome, this action is contained in his concept, for we have supposed that it is the nature of such a perfect concept of a subject to involve everything, in fact so that the predicate may be included in the subject *ut possit inesse subjecto*. We may say that it is not in virtue of this concept or idea that he is obliged to perform this action, since it pertains to him only because God knows everything. But it will be insisted in reply that his nature or form responds to this concept, and since God imposes upon him this personality, he is compelled henceforth to live up to it. I could reply by instancing the similar case of the future contingencies which as yet have no reality save in the understanding and will of God, and which, because God has given them in advance this form, must needs correspond to it. But I prefer to overcome a difficulty rather than to excuse it by instancing other difficulties, and what I am about to say will serve to clear up the one as well as the other. It is here that must be applied the distinction in the kind of relation, and I say that that which happens conformably to these decrees is assured, but that it is not therefore necessary, and if anyone did the contrary, he would do nothing impossible in itself, although it is impossible *ex hypothesi* that that other happen. For if anyone were capable of carrying out a complete demonstration by virtue of which he could prove this connection of the subject, which is Caesar, with the predicate, which is his successful enterprise, he would bring us to see in fact that the future dictatorship of Caesar had its basis in his concept or nature, so that one would see there a reason why he resolved to cross the Rubicon rather than to stop, and why he gained instead of losing the day at Pharsalus, and that it was reasonable and by consequence assured that this would occur, but one would not prove that it was necessary in itself, nor that the contrary implied a contradiction, almost in the same way in which it is reasonable and assured that God will always do what is best although that which is less perfect is not thereby implied. For it would be found that this demonstration of this predicate as belonging to Caesar is not as absolute as are those of numbers or of geometry, but that this predicate supposes a sequence of things which God has shown by his free will. This sequence is based on the first free decree of God which was to do always that which is the most perfect and upon the decree which God made following the first one, regarding human nature, which is that men should always do, although freely, that which appears to be the best. Now every truth which is founded upon this kind of decree is contingent, although certain, for the decrees of God do not change the possibilities of things and, as I have already said, although God assuredly chooses the best, this does not prevent that which is less perfect from being possible in itself. Although it will never happen, it is not its impossibility but its imperfection which causes him to reject it. Now nothing is necessitated whose opposite is possible. One will then be in a position to satisfy these kinds of difficulties, however great they may appear (and in fact they have not been less vexing to all other thinkers who have ever treated this matter), provided that he considers well that all contingent propositions have reasons why they are thus, rather than otherwise, or indeed (what is the same thing) that they have proof *a priori* of their truth, which render them certain and show that the connection of the subject and predicate in these propositions has its basis in the nature of the one and of the other, but he must further remember that such contingent propositions have not the demonstrations of necessity, since their reasons are founded only on the principle of contingency or of the existence of things, that is to say, upon that which is, or which appears to be the best among several things equally possible. Necessary truths, on the other hand, are founded upon the principle of contradiction, and upon the possibility or impossibility of the essences themselves, without regard here to the free will of God or of creatures.

XIV. God produces different substances according to the different views which he has of the world, and by the intervention of God, the appropriate nature of each substance brings it about that what happens to one corresponds to what happens to all the others, without, however, their acting upon one another directly.

After having seen, to a certain extent, in what the nature of substances consists, we must try to explain the dependence they have upon one another and their actions and passions. Now it is first of all very evident that created substances depend upon God who preserves them and can produce them continually by a kind of emanation just as we produce our thoughts, for when God turns, so to say, on all sides and in all fashions, the general system of phenomena which he finds it good to produce for the sake of manifesting his glory, and when he regards all the aspects of the world in all possible manners, since there is no relation which escapes his omniscience, the result of each view of the universe as seen from a different position is a substance which expresses the universe conformably to this view, provided God sees fit to render his thought effective and to produce the substance, and since God's vision is always true, our perceptions are always true and that which deceives us are our judgments, which are of us. Now we have said before, and it follows from what we have just said that each substance is a world by itself, independent of everything else excepting God; therefore, all our phenomena that is all things which are ever able to happen to us, are only consequences of our being. Now as the phenomena maintain a certain order conformably to our nature, or so to speak to the world which is in us (from whence it follows that we can, for the regulation of our conduct, make useful observations which are justified by the outcome of the future phenomena) and as we are thus able often to judge the future by the past without deceiving ourselves, we have sufficient grounds for saying that these phenomena are true and we will not be put to the task of inquiring whether they are outside of us, and whether others perceive them also.

Nevertheless it is most true that the perceptions and expressions of all substances intercorrespond, so that each one following independently certain reasons or laws which he has noticed meets others which are doing the same, as when several have agreed to meet together in a certain place on a set day, they are able to carry out the plan if they wish. Now although all express the same phenomena, this does not bring it about that their expressions are exactly alike. It is sufficient if they are proportional. As when several spectators think they see the same thing and are agreed about it, although each one sees or speaks according to the measure of his vision. It is God alone, (from whom all individuals emanate continually, and who sees the universe not only as they see it, but besides in a very different way from them) who is the cause of this correspondence in their phenomena and who brings it about that that which is particular to one, is also common to all, otherwise there would be no relation. In a way, then, we might properly say, although it seems strange, that a particular substance never acts upon another particular substance nor is it acted upon by it. That which happens to each one is only the consequence of its complete idea or concept, since this idea already includes all the predicates and expresses the whole universe. In fact nothing can happen to us except thoughts and perceptions, and all our thoughts and perceptions are but the consequence, contingent it is true, of our precedent thoughts and perceptions, in such a way that were I able to consider directly all that happens or appears to me at the present time, I should be able to see all that will happen to me or that will ever appear to me. This future will not fail me, and will surely appear to me even if all that which is outside of me were destroyed, save only that God and myself were left.

Since, however, we ordinarily attribute to other things an action upon us which brings us to perceive things in a certain manner, it is necessary to consider the basis of this judgment and to inquire what there is of truth in it.

XV. The action of one finite substance upon another consists only in the increase in the degrees of the expression of the first combined with a decrease in that of the second, in so far as God has in advance fashioned them so that they shall act in accord.

Without entering into a long discussion it is sufficient for reconciling the language of metaphysics with that of practical life to remark that we preferably attribute to ourselves, and with reason, the phenomena which we express the most perfectly, and that we attribute to other substances those phenomena which each one expresses the best. Thus a substance, which is of an infinite extension in so far as it expresses all, becomes limited in proportion to its more or less perfect manner of expression. It is thus then that we may conceive of substances as interfering with and limiting one another, and hence we are able to say that in this sense they act upon one another, and that they, so to speak, accommodate themselves to one another. For it can happen that a single change which augments the expression of the one may diminish that of the other. Now the virtue of a particular substance is to express well the glory of God, and the better it expresses it, the less is it limited. Everything when it expresses its virtue of power, that is to say, when it acts, changes to better, and expands just in so far as it acts. When therefore a change occurs by which several substances are affected (in fact every change affects them all) I think we may say that those substances, which by this change pass immediately to a greater degree of perfection, or to a more perfect expression, exert power and act, while those which pass to a lesser degree disclose their weakness and suffer. I also hold that every activity of a substance which has perception implies some pleasure, and every passion some pain, except that it may very well happen that a present advantage will be eventually destroyed by a greater evil, whence it comes that one may sin in acting or exerting his power and in finding pleasure.

XVI. The extraordinary intervention of God is not excluded in that which our particular essences express, because their expression includes everything. Such intervention, however, goes beyond the power of our natural being or of our distinct expression, because these are finite, and follow certain subordinate regulations.

There remains for us at present only to explain how it is possible that God has influence at times upon men or upon other substances by an extraordinary or miraculous intervention, since it seems that nothing is able to happen which is extraordinary or supernatural in as much as all the events which occur to the other substances are only the consequences of their natures. We must recall what was said above in regard to the miracles in the universe. These always conform to the universal law of the general order, although they may contravene the subordinate regulations, and since every person or substance is like a little world which expresses the great world, we can say that this extraordinary action of God upon this substance is nevertheless miraculous, although it is comprised in the general order of the universe in so far as it is expressed by the individual essence or concept of this substance. This is why, if we understand in our natures all that they express, nothing is supernatural in them, because they reach out to everything, an effect always expressing its cause, and God being the veritable cause of the substances. But as that which our natures express the most perfectly pertains to them in a particular manner, that being their special power, and since they are limited, as I have just explained, many things there are which surpass the powers of our natures and even of all limited natures. As a consequence, to speak more clearly, I say that the miracles and the extraordinary interventions of God have this peculiarity that they cannot be foreseen by any created mind however enlightened. This is because the distinct comprehension of the fundamental order surpasses them all, while on the other hand, that which is called natural depends upon less fundamental regulations which the creatures are able to understand. In order then that my words may be as irreprehensible as the meaning I am trying to convey, it will be well to associate certain words with certain significations. We may call that which includes everything that we express and which expresses our union with God himself, nothing going beyond it, our essence. But that which is limited in us may be designated as our nature or our power and in accordance with this terminology that which goes beyond the natures of all created substances is supernatural.

XVII. An example of a subordinate regulation in the law of nature which demonstrates that God always preserves the same amount of force but not the same quantity of motion:—against the Cartesians and many others.

I have frequently spoken of subordinate regulations, or of the laws of nature, and it seems that it will be well to give an example. Our new philosophers are unanimous in employing that famous law that God always preserves the same amount of motion in the universe. In fact it is a very plausible law, and in times past I held it for indubitable. But since then I have learned in what its fault consists. Monsieur Descartes and many other clever mathematicians have thought that the quantity of motion, that is to say the velocity multiplied by the mass[9] of the moving body, is exactly equivalent to the moving force, or to speak in mathematical terms that the force varies as the velocity multiplied by the mass. Now it is reasonable that the same force is always preserved in the universe. So also, looking to phenomena, it will be readily seen that a mechanical perpetual motion is impossible, because the force in such a machine, being always diminished a little by friction and so ultimately destined to be entirely spent, would necessarily have to recoup its losses, and consequently would keep on increasing of itself without any new impulsion from without; and we see furthermore that the force of a body is diminished only in proportion as it gives up force, either to a contiguous body or to its own parts, in so far as they have a separate movement. The mathematicians to whom I have referred think that what can be said of force can be said of the quantity of motion. In order, however, to show the difference I make two suppositions: in the first place, that a body falling from a certain height acquires a force enabling it to remount to the same height, provided that its direction is turned that way, or provided that there are no hindrances. For instance, a pendulum will rise exactly to the height from which it has fallen, provided the resistance of the air and of certain other small particles do not diminish a little its acquired force.

---

[9] This term is employed here for the sake of clearness. Leibniz did not possess the concept "mass," which was enunciated by Newton in the same year in which the present treatise was written, 1686. Leibniz uses the terms "body," "magnitude of body," etc. The technical expression "mass" occurs once only in the writings of Leibniz (in a treatise published in 1695), and was there doubtless borrowed from Newton. For the history of the controversy concerning the Cartesian and Leibnizian measure of force, see Mach's *Science of Mechanics*, Chicago, 1893, pp. 272 et seq.—Trans.

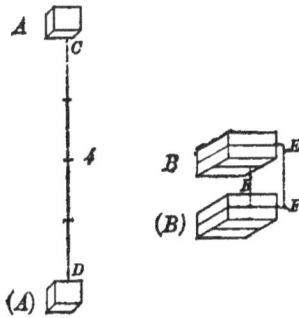

I suppose in the second place that it will take as much force to lift a body A weighing one pound to the height CD, four feet, as to raise a body B weighing four pounds to the height EF, one foot. These two suppositions are granted by our new philosophers. It is therefore manifest that the body A falling from the height CD acquires exactly as much force as the body B falling from the height EF, for the body B at F, having by the first supposition sufficient force to return to E, has therefore the force to carry a body of four pounds to the distance of one foot, EF. And likewise the body A at D, having the force to return to C, has also the force required to carry a body weighing one pound, its own weight, back to C, a distance of four feet. Now by the second supposition the force of these two bodies is equal. Let us now see if the quantity of motion is the same in each case. It is here that we will be surprised to find a very great difference, for it has been proved by Galileo that the velocity acquired by the fall CD is double the velocity acquired by the fall EF, although the height is four times as great. Multiplying, therefore, the body A, whose mass is 1, by its velocity, which is 2, the product or the quantity of movement will be 2, and on the other hand, if we multiply the body B, whose mass is 4, by its velocity, which is 1, the product or quantity of motion will be 4. Hence the quantity of the motion of the body A at the point D is half the quantity of motion of the body B at the point F, yet their forces are equal, and there is therefore a great difference between the quantity of motion and the force. This is what we set out to show. We can see therefore how the force ought to be estimated by the quantity of the effect which it is able to produce, for example by the height to which a body of certain weight can be raised. This is a very different thing from the velocity which can be imparted to it, and in order to impart to it double the velocity we must have double the force. Nothing is simpler than this proof and Monsieur Descartes has fallen into error here, only because he trusted too much to his thoughts even when they had not been ripened by reflection. But it astonishes me that his disciples have not noticed this error, and I am afraid that they are beginning to imitate little by little certain Peripatetics whom they ridicule, and that they are accustoming themselves to consult rather the books of their master, than reason or nature.

XVIII. The distinction between force and the quantity of motion is, among other reasons, important as showing that we must have recourse to metaphysical considerations in addition to discussions of extension if we wish to explain the phenomena of matter.

This consideration of the force, distinguished from the quantity of motion is of importance, not only in physics and mechanics for finding the real laws of nature and the principles of motion, and even for correcting many practical errors which have crept into the writings of certain able mathematicians, but also in metaphysics it is of importance for the better understanding of principles. Because motion, if we regard only its exact and formal meaning, that is, change of place, is not something entirely real, and when several bodies change their places reciprocally, it is not possible to determine by considering the bodies alone to which among them movement or repose is to be attributed, as I could demonstrate geometrically, if I wished to stop for it now. But the force, or the proximate cause of these changes is something more real, and there are sufficient grounds for attributing it to one body rather than to another, and it is only through this latter investigation that we can determine to which one the movement must appertain. Now this force is something different from size, from form or from motion, and it can be seen from this consideration that the whole meaning of a body is not exhausted in its extension together with its modifications as our moderns persuade themselves. We are therefore obliged to restore certain beings or forms which they have banished. It appears more and more clear that although all the particular phenomena of nature can be explained mathematically or mechanically by those who understand them, yet nevertheless, the general principles of corporeal nature and even of mechanics are metaphysical rather than geometric, and belong rather to certain indivisible forms or natures as the causes of the appearances, than to the corporeal mass or to extension. This reflection is able to reconcile the mechanical philosophy of the moderns with the circumspection of those intelligent and well-meaning persons who, with a certain justice, fear that we are becoming too far removed from immaterial beings and that we are thus prejudicing piety.

XIX. The utility of final causes in Physics.

As I do not wish to judge people in ill part I bring no accusation against our new philosophers who pretend to banish final causes from physics, but I am nevertheless obliged to avow that the consequences of such a banishment appear to me dangerous, especially when joined to that position which I refuted at the beginning of this treatise. That position seemed to go the length of discarding final causes entirely as though God proposed no end and no good in his activity, or as if good were not to be the object of his will. I hold on the contrary that it is just in this that the principle of all existences and of the laws of nature must be sought, hence God always proposes the best and most perfect. I am quite willing to grant that we are liable to err when we wish to determine the purposes or councils of God, but this is the case only when we try to limit them to some particular design, thinking that he has had in view only a single thing, while in fact he regards everything at once. As for instance, if we think that God has made the world only for us, it is a great blunder, although it may be quite true that he has made it entirely for us, and that there is nothing in the universe which does not touch us and which does not accommodate itself to the regard which he has for us according to the principle laid down above. Therefore when we see some good effect or some perfection which happens or which follows from the works of God we are able to say assuredly that God has purposed it, for he does nothing by chance, and is not like us who sometimes fail to do well. Therefore, far from being able to fall into error in this respect as do the extreme statesmen who postulate too much foresight in the designs of Princes, or as do commentators who seek for too much erudition in their authors, it will be impossible to attribute too much reflection to God's infinite wisdom, and there is no matter in which error is less to be feared provided we confine ourselves to affirmations and provided we avoid negative statements which limit the designs of God. All those who see the admirable structure of animals find themselves led to recognize the wisdom of the author of things and I advise those who have any sentiment of piety and indeed of true philosophy to hold aloof from the expressions of certain pretentious minds who instead of saying that eyes were made for seeing, say that we see because we find ourselves having eyes. When one seriously holds such opinions which hand everything over to material necessity or to a kind of chance (although either alternative ought to appear ridiculous to those who understand what we have explained above) it is difficult to recognize an intelligent author of nature. The effect should correspond to its cause and indeed it is best known through the recognition of its cause, so that it is reasonable to introduce a sovereign intelligence ordering things, and in place of making use of the wisdom of this sovereign being, to employ only the properties of matter to explain phenomena. As if in order to account for the capture of an important place by a prince, the historian should say it was because the particles of powder in the cannon having been touched by a spark of fire expanded with a rapidity capable of pushing a hard solid body against the walls of the place, while the little particles which composed the brass of the cannon were so well interlaced that they did not separate under this impact,—as if he should account for it in this way instead of making us see how the foresight of the conqueror brought him to choose the time and the proper means and how his ability surmounted all obstacles.

XX. A noteworthy disquisition in Plato's Phaedo against the philosophers who were too materialistic.

This reminds me of a fine disquisition by Socrates in Plato's Phaedo, which agrees perfectly with my opinion on this subject and seems to have been uttered expressly for our too materialistic philosophers. This agreement has led me to a desire to translate it although it is a little long. Perhaps this example will give some of us an incentive to share in many of the other beautiful and well balanced thoughts which are found in the writings of this famous author.[10]

XXI. If the mechanical laws depended upon Geometry alone without metaphysical influences, the phenomena would be very different from what they are.

Now since the wisdom of God has always been recognized in the detail of the mechanical structures of certain particular bodies, it should also be shown in the general economy of the world and in the constitution of the laws of nature. This is so true that even in the laws of motion in general, the plans of this wisdom have been noticed. For if bodies were only extended masses, and motion were only a change of place, and if everything ought to be and could be deduced by geometric necessity from these two definitions alone, it would follow, as I have shown elsewhere, that the smallest body on contact with a very large one at rest would impart to it its own velocity, yet without losing any of the velocity that it had. A quantity of other rules wholly contrary to the formation of a system would also have to be admitted. But the decree of the divine wisdom in preserving always the same force and the same total direction has provided for a system. I find indeed that many of the effects of nature can be accounted for in a twofold way, that is to say

---

[10] There is a gap here in the MS., intended for the passage from Plato, the translation of which Leibniz did not supply.—Trans.

by a consideration of efficient causes, and again independently by a consideration of final causes. An example of the latter is God's decree to always carry out his plan by the easiest and most determined way. I have shown this elsewhere in accounting for the catoptric and dioptric laws, and I will speak more at length about it in what follows.

XXII. Reconciliation of the two methods of explanation, the one using final causes, and the other efficient causes, thus satisfying both those who explain nature mechanically and those who have recourse to incorporeal natures.

It is worth while to make the preceding remark in order to reconcile those who hope to explain mechanically the formation of the first tissue of an animal and all the interrelation of the parts, with those who account for the same structure by referring to final causes. Both explanations are good; both are useful not only for the admiring of the work of a great artificer, but also for the discovery of useful facts in physics and medicine. And writers who take these diverse routes should not speak ill of each other. For I see that those who attempt to explain beauty by the divine anatomy ridicule those who imagine that the apparently fortuitous flow of certain liquids has been able to produce such a beautiful variety and that they regard them as overbold and irreverent. These others on the contrary treat the former as simple and superstitious, and compare them to those ancients who regarded the physicists as impious when they maintained that not Jupiter thundered but some material which is found in the clouds. The best plan would be to join the two ways of thinking. To use a practical comparison, we recognize and praise the ability of a workman not only when we show what designs he had in making the parts of his machine, but also when we explain the instruments which he employed in making each part, above all if these instruments are simple and ingeniously contrived. God is also a workman able enough to produce a machine still a thousand times more ingenious than is our body, by employing only certain quite simple liquids purposely composed in such a way that ordinary laws of nature alone are required to develop them so as to produce such a marvelous effect. But it is also true that this development would not take place if God were not the author of nature. Yet I find that the method of efficient causes, which goes much deeper and is in a measure more immediate and *a priori*, is also more difficult when we come to details, and I think that our philosophers are still very frequently far removed from making the most of this method. The method of final causes, however, is easier and can be frequently employed to find out important and useful truths which we should have to seek for a long time, if we were confined to that other more physical method of which anatomy is able to furnish many examples. It seems to me that Snellius, who was the first discoverer of the laws of refraction would have waited a long time before finding them if he had wished to seek out first how light was formed. But he apparently followed that method which the ancients employed for Catoptrics, that is, the method of final causes. Because, while seeking for the easiest way in which to conduct a ray of light from one given point to another given point by reflection from a given plane (supposing that that was the design of nature) they discovered the equality of the angles of incidence and reflection, as can be seen from a little treatise by Heliodorus of Larissa and also elsewhere. This principle Mons. Snellius, I believe, and afterwards independently of him, M. Fermat, applied most ingeniously to refraction. For since the rays while in the same media always maintain the same proportion of sines, which in turn corresponds to the resistance of the media, it appears that they follow the easiest way, or at least that way which is the most determinate for passing from a given point in one medium to a given point in another medium. That demonstration of this same theorem which M. Descartes has given, using efficient causes, is much less satisfactory. At least we have grounds to think that he would never have found the principle by that means if he had not learned in Holland of the discovery of Snellius.

XXIII. Returning to immaterial substances we explain how God acts upon the understanding of spirits and ask whether one always keeps the idea of what he thinks about.

I have thought it well to insist a little upon final causes, upon incorporeal natures and upon an intelligent cause with respect to bodies so as to show the use of these conceptions in physics and in mathematics. This for two reasons, first to purge from mechanical philosophy the impiety that is imputed to it, second, to elevate to nobler lines of thought the thinking of our philosophers who incline to materialistic considerations alone. Now, however, it will be well to return from corporeal substances to the consideration of immaterial natures and particularly of spirits, and to speak of the methods which God uses to enlighten them and to act upon them. Although we must not forget that there are here at the same time certain laws of nature in regard to which I can speak more amply elsewhere. It will be enough for now to touch upon ideas and to inquire if we see everything in God and how God is our light. First of all it will be in place to remark that the wrong use of ideas occasions many errors. For when one reasons in regard to anything, he imagines that he has an idea of it and this is the foundation upon which certain philosophers, ancient and modern, have constructed a demonstration of God that is extremely imperfect. It must be, they say, that I have an idea of God, or of a perfect being, since I think of him and we cannot think without having ideas; now the idea of this being includes all perfections and since existence is one of these perfections, it follows that he exists. But I reply, inasmuch as we often think of impossible chimeras, for example of the highest degree of swiftness, of the greatest number, of the meeting of the conchoid with its base or determinant, such reasoning is not sufficient. It is therefore in this sense that we can say that there are true and false ideas according as the thing which is in question is possible or not. And it is when he is assured of the possibility of a thing, that one can boast of having an idea of it. Therefore, the aforesaid argument proves that God exists, if he is possible. This is in fact an excellent privilege of the divine nature, to have need only of a possibility or an essence in order to actually exist, and it is just this which is called *ens a se*.

XXIV. What clear and obscure, distinct and confused, adequate and inadequate, intuitive and assumed knowledge is, and the definition of nominal, real, causal and essential.

In order to understand better the nature of ideas it is necessary to touch somewhat upon the various kinds of knowledge. When I am able to recognize a thing among others, without being able to say in what its differences or characteristics consist, the knowledge is confused. Sometimes indeed we may know clearly, that is without being in the slightest doubt, that a poem or a picture is well or badly done because there is in it an "I know not what" which satisfies or shocks us. Such knowledge is not yet distinct. It is when I am able to explain the peculiarities which a thing has, that the knowledge is called distinct. Such is the knowledge of an assayer who discerns the true gold from the false by means of certain proofs or marks which make up the definition of gold. But distinct knowledge has degrees, because ordinarily the conceptions which enter into the definitions will themselves have need of definition, and are only known confusedly. When at length everything which enters into a definition or into distinct knowledge is known distinctly, even back to the primitive conception, I call that knowledge adequate. When my mind understands at once and distinctly all the primitive ingredients of a conception, then we have intuitive knowledge. This is extremely rare as most human knowledge is only confused or indeed assumed. It is well also to distinguish nominal from real definition. I call a definition nominal when there is doubt whether an exact conception of it is possible; as for instance, when I say that an endless screw is a line in three dimensional space whose parts are congruent or fall one upon another. Now although this is one of the reciprocal properties of an endless screw, he who did not know from elsewhere what an endless screw was could doubt if such a line were possible, because the other lines whose ends are congruent (there are only two: the circumference of a circle and the straight line) are plane figures, that is to say they can be described *in plano*. This instance enables us to see that any reciprocal property can serve as a nominal definition, but when the property brings us to see the possibility of a thing it makes the definition real, and as long as one has only a nominal definition he cannot be sure of the consequences which he draws, because if it conceals a contradiction or an impossibility he would be able to draw the opposite conclusions. That is why truths do not depend upon names and are not arbitrary, as some of our new philosophers think. There is also a considerable difference among real definitions, for when the possibility proves itself only by experience, as in the definition of quicksilver, whose possibility we know because such a body, which is both an extremely heavy fluid and quite volatile, actually exists, the definition is merely real and nothing more. If, however, the proof of the possibility is *a priori*, the definition is not only real but also causal as for instance when it contains the possible generation of a thing. Finally when the definition, without assuming anything which requires a proof *a priori* of its possibility, carries the analysis clear to the primitive conception, the definition is perfect or essential.

XXV. In what cases knowledge is added to mere contemplation of the idea.

Now it is manifest that we have no idea of a conception when it is impossible. And in case the knowledge, where we have the idea of it, is only assumed, we do not visualize it because such a conception is known only in like manner as conceptions internally impossible. And if it be in fact possible, it is not by this kind of knowledge that we learn its possibility. For instance, when I am thinking of a thousand or of a chiliagon, I frequently do it without contemplating the idea. Even if I say a thousand is ten times a hundred, I frequently do not trouble to think what ten and a hundred are, because I assume that I know, and I do not consider it necessary to stop just at present to conceive of them. Therefore it may well happen, as it in fact does happen often enough, that I am mistaken in regard to a conception which I assume that I understand, although it is an impossible truth or at least is incompatible with others with which I join it, and whether I am mistaken or not, this way of assuming our knowledge remains the same. It is, then, only when our knowledge is clear in regard to confused conceptions, and when it is intuitive in regard to those which are distinct, that we see its entire idea.

XXVI. Ideas are all stored up within us. Plato's doctrine of reminiscence.

In order to see clearly what an idea is, we must guard ourselves against a misunderstanding. Many regard the idea as the form or the differentiation of our thinking, and according to this opinion we have the idea in our mind, in so far as we are thinking of it, and each separate time that we think of it anew we have another idea although similar to the preceding one. Some, however, take the idea as the immediate object of thought, or as a permanent form which remains even when we are no longer contemplating it. As a matter of fact our soul has the power of representing to itself any form or nature whenever the occasion comes for thinking about it, and I think that this activity of our soul is, so far as it expresses some nature, form or essence, properly the idea of the thing. This is in us, and is always in us, whether we are thinking of it or no. (Our soul expresses God and the universe and all essences as well as all existences.) This position is in accord with my principles that naturally nothing enters into our minds from outside.

It is a bad habit we have of thinking as though our minds receive certain messengers, as it were, or as if they had doors or windows. We have in our minds all those forms for all periods of time because the mind at every moment expresses all its future thoughts and already thinks confusedly of all that of which it will ever think distinctly. Nothing can be taught us of which we have not already in our minds the idea. This idea is as it were the material out of which the thought will form itself. This is what Plato has excellently brought out in his doctrine of reminiscence, a doctrine which contains a great deal of truth, provided that it is properly understood and purged of the error of pre-existence, and provided that one does not conceive of the soul as having already known and thought at some other time what it learns and thinks now. Plato has also confirmed his position by a beautiful experiment. He introduces a small boy, whom he leads by short steps, to extremely difficult truths of geometry bearing on incommensurables, all this without teaching the boy anything, merely drawing out replies by a well arranged series of questions. This shows that the soul virtually knows those things, and needs only to be reminded (animadverted) to recognize the truths. Consequently it possesses at least the idea upon which those truths depend. We may say even that it already possesses those truths, if we consider them as the relations of the ideas.

XXVII. In what respect our souls can be compared to blank tablets and
how conceptions are derived from the senses.

Aristotle preferred to compare our souls to blank tablets prepared
for writing, and he maintained that nothing is in the understanding
which does not come through the senses. This position is in accord with
the popular conceptions as Aristotle's positions usually are. Plato
thinks more profoundly. Such tenets or practicologies are nevertheless
allowable in ordinary use somewhat in the same way as those who
accept the Copernican theory still continue to speak of the rising and
setting of the sun. I find indeed that these usages can be given a real
meaning containing no error, quite in the same way as I have already
pointed out that we may truly say particular substances act upon one
another. In this same sense we may say that knowledge is received
from without through the medium of the senses because certain exterior
things contain or express more particularly the causes which determine
us to certain thoughts. Because in the ordinary uses of life we attribute
to the soul only that which belongs to it most manifestly and
particularly, and there is no advantage in going further. When,
however, we are dealing with the exactness of metaphysical truths, it is
important to recognize the powers and independence of the soul which
extend infinitely further than is commonly supposed. In order,
therefore, to avoid misunderstandings it would be well to choose
separate terms for the two. These expressions which are in the soul
whether one is conceiving of them or not may be called ideas, while
those which one conceives of or constructs may be called conceptions,
conceptus. But whatever terms are used, it is always false to say that all
our conceptions come from the so-called external senses, because those
conceptions which I have of myself and of my thoughts, and
consequently of being, of substance, of action, of identity, and of many
others came from an inner experience.

XXVIII. The only immediate object of our perceptions which exists
outside of us is God, and in him alone is our light.

In the strictly metaphysical sense no external cause acts upon us
excepting God alone, and he is in immediate relation with us only by
virtue of our continual dependence upon him. Whence it follows that
there is absolutely no other external object which comes into contact
with our souls and directly excites perceptions in us. We have in our
souls ideas of everything, only because of the continual action of God
upon us, that is to say, because every effect expresses its cause and
therefore the essences of our souls are certain expressions, imitations or
images of the divine essence, divine thought and divine will, including

all the ideas which are there contained. We may say, therefore, that God is for us the only immediate external object, and that we see things through him. For example, when we see the sun or the stars, it is God who gives to us and preserves in us the ideas and whenever our senses are affected according to his own laws in a certain manner, it is he, who by his continual concurrence, determines our thinking. God is the sun and the light of souls, *lumen illuminans omnem hominem venientem in hunc mundum*, although this is not the current conception. I think I have already remarked that during the scholastic period many believed God to be the light of the soul, *intellectus agens animæ rationalis*, following in this the Holy Scriptures and the fathers who were always more Platonic than Aristotelian in their mode of thinking. The Averroists misused this conception, but others, among whom were several mystic theologians, and William of Saint Amour, also I think, understood this conception in a manner which assured the dignity of God and was able to raise the soul to a knowledge of its welfare.

XXIX. Yet we think directly by means of our own ideas and not through God's.

Nevertheless I cannot approve of the position of certain able philosophers who seem to hold that our ideas themselves are in God and not at all in us. I think that in taking this position they have neither sufficiently considered the nature of substance, which we have just explained, nor the entire extension and independence of the soul which includes all that happens to it, and expresses God, and with him all possible and actual beings in the same way that an effect expresses its cause. It is indeed inconceivable that the soul should think using the ideas of something else. The soul when it thinks of anything must be affected effectively in a certain manner, and it must needs have in itself in advance not only the passive capacity of being thus affected, a capacity already wholly determined, but it must have besides an active power by virtue of which it has always had in its nature the marks of the future production of this thought, and the disposition to produce it at its proper time. All of this shows that the soul already includes the idea which is comprised in any particular thought.

XXX. How God inclines our souls without necessitating them; that there are no grounds for complaint; that we must not ask why Judas sinned because this free act is contained in his concept, the only question being why Judas the sinner is admitted to existence, preferably to other possible persons; concerning the original imperfection, or limitation before the fall and concerning the different degrees of grace.

Regarding the action of God upon the human will there are many quite different considerations which it would take too long to investigate here. Nevertheless the following is what can be said in general. God in co-operating with ordinary actions only follows the laws which he has established, that is to say, he continually preserves and produces our being so that the ideas come to us spontaneously or with freedom in that order which the concept of our individual substance carries with itself. In this concept they can be foreseen for all eternity. Furthermore, by virtue of the decree which God has made that the will shall always seek the apparent good in certain particular respects (in regard to which this apparent good always has in it something of reality expressing or imitating God's will), he, without at all necessitating our choice, determines it by that which appears most desirable. For absolutely speaking, our will as contrasted with necessity, is in a state of indifference, being able to act otherwise, or wholly to suspend its action, either alternative being and remaining possible. It therefore devolves upon the soul to be on guard against appearances, by means of a firm will, to reflect and to refuse to act or decide in certain circumstances, except after mature deliberation. It is, however, true and has been assured from all eternity that certain souls will not employ their power upon certain occasions.

But who could do more than God has done, and can such a soul complain of anything except itself? All these complaints after the deed are unjust, inasmuch as they would have been unjust before the deed. Would this soul a little before committing the sin have had the right to complain of God as though he had determined the sin. Since the determinations of God in these matters cannot be foreseen, how would the soul know that it was preordained to sin unless it had already committed the sin? It is merely a question of wishing to or not wishing to, and God could not have set an easier or juster condition. Therefore all judges without asking the reasons which have disposed a man to have an evil will, consider only how far this will is wrong. But, you object, perhaps it is ordained from all eternity that I will sin. Find your own answer. Perhaps it has not been. Now then, without asking for what you are unable to know and in regard to which you can have no light, act according to your duty and your knowledge. But, some one will object; whence comes it then that this man will assuredly do this sin? The reply is easy. It is that otherwise he would not be a man. For God foresees from all time that there will be a certain Judas, and in the concept or idea of him which God has, is contained this future free act. The only question, therefore, which remains is why this certain Judas, the betrayer who is possible only because of the idea of God, actually exists. To this question, however, we can expect no answer here on earth excepting to say in general that it is because God has found it good that he should exist notwithstanding that sin which he foresaw. This evil will be more than overbalanced. God will derive a greater good from it, and it will finally turn out that this series of events in which is included the existence of this sinner, is the most perfect among all the possible series of events. An explanation in every case of the admirable economy of this choice cannot be given while we are sojourners on earth. It is enough to know the excellence without understanding it. It is here that must be recognized *altitudinem divitiarum*, the unfathomable depth of the divine wisdom, without hesitating at a detail which involves an infinite number of considerations. It is clear, however, that God is not the cause of ill. For not only after the loss of innocence by men, has original sin possessed the soul, but even before that there was an original limitation or imperfection in the very nature of all creatures, which rendered them open to sin and able to fall. There is, therefore, no more difficulty in the supralapsarian view than there is in the other views of sin. To this also, it seems to me can be reduced the opinion of Saint Augustine and of other authors: that the root of evil is in the negativity, that is to say, in the lack or limitation of creatures which God graciously remedies by whatever degree of perfection it pleases him to give. This grace of God, whether ordinary or extraordinary has its degrees and its measures. It is always efficacious in itself to produce a certain proportionate effect and furthermore it is always sufficient not only to keep one from sin but even to effect his salvation, provided that the man co-operates with that which is in him. It has not always, however, sufficient power to overcome the inclination, for, if it did, it would no longer be limited in any way, and this superiority to limitations is reserved to that unique grace which is absolutely efficacious. This grace is always victorious whether through its own self or through the congruity of circumstances.

XXXI. Concerning the motives of election; concerning faith foreseen
and the absolute decree and that it all reduces to the question why
God has chosen and resolved to admit to existence just such a
possible person, whose concept includes just such a sequence of
free acts and of free gifts of grace. This at once puts an end to all
difficulties.

Finally, the grace of God is wholly unprejudiced and creatures
have no claim upon it. Just as it is not sufficient in accounting for
God's choice in his dispensations of grace to refer to his absolute or
conditional prevision of men's future actions, so it is also wrong to
imagine his decrees as absolute with no reasonable motive. As concerns
foreseen faith and good works, it is very true that God has elected none
but those whose faith and charity he foresees, *quos se fide donaturum
praescivit*. The same question, however, arises again as to why God
gives to some rather than to others the grace of faith or of good works.
As concerns God's ability to foresee not only the faith and good deeds,
but also their material and predisposition, or that which a man on his
part contributes to them (since there are as truly diversities on the part
of men as on the part of grace, and a man although he needs to be
aroused to good and needs to become converted, yet acts in accordance
with his temperament),—as regards his ability to foresee there are
many who say that God, knowing what a particular man will do
without grace, that is without his extraordinary assistance, or knowing
at least what will be the human contribution, resolves to give grace to
those whose natural dispositions are the best, or at any rate are the least
imperfect and evil. But if this were the case then the natural
dispositions in so far as they were good would be like gifts of grace,
since God would have given advantages to some over others; and
therefore, since he would well know that the natural advantages which
he had given would serve as motives for his grace or for his
extraordinary assistance, would not everything be reduced to his
mercy? I think, therefore, that since we do not know how much and in
what way God regards natural dispositions in the dispensations of his
grace, it would be safest and most exact to say, in accordance with our
principles and as I have already remarked, that there must needs be
among possible beings the person Peter or John whose concept or idea
contains all that particular sequence of ordinary and extraordinary
manifestations of grace together with the rest of the accompanying
events and circumstances, and that it has pleased God to choose him
among an infinite number of persons equally possible for actual
existence. When we have said this there seems nothing left to ask, and
all difficulties vanish. For in regard to that great and ultimate question
why it has pleased God to choose him among so great a number of

possible persons, it is surely unreasonable to demand more than the general reasons which we have given. The reasons in detail surpass our ken. Therefore, instead of postulating an absolute decree, which being without reason would be unreasonable, and instead of postulating reasons which do not succeed in solving the difficulties and in turn have need themselves of reasons, it will be best to say with St. Paul that there are for God's choice certain great reasons of wisdom and congruity which he follows, which reasons, however, are unknown to mortals and are founded upon the general order, whose goal is the greatest perfection of the world. This is what is meant when the motives of God's glory and of the manifestation of his justice are spoken of, as well as when men speak of his mercy, and his perfection in general; that immense vastness of wealth, in fine, with which the soul of the same St. Paul was so thrilled.

XXXII. Usefulness of these principles in matters of piety and of religion.

In addition it seems that the thoughts which we have just explained and particularly the great principle of the perfection of God's operations and the concept of substance which includes all its changes with all its accompanying circumstances, far from injuring, serve rather to confirm religion, serve to dissipate great difficulties, to inflame souls with a divine love and to raise the mind to a knowledge of incorporeal substances much more than the present-day hypotheses. For it appears clearly that all other substances depend upon God just as our thoughts emanate from our own substances; that God is all in all and that he is intimately united to all created things, in proportion however to their perfection; that it is he alone who determines them from without by his influence, and if to act is to determine directly, it may be said in metaphysical language that God alone acts upon me and he alone causes me to do good or ill, other substances contributing only because of his determinations; because God, who takes all things into consideration, distributes his bounties and compels created beings to accommodate themselves to one another. Thus God alone constitutes the relation or communication between substances. It is through him that the phenomena of the one meet and accord with the phenomena of the others, so that there may be a reality in our perceptions. In common parlance, however, an action is attributed to particular causes in the sense that I have explained above because it is not necessary to make continual mention of the universal cause when speaking of particular cases. It can be seen also that every substance has a perfect spontaneity (which becomes liberty with intelligent substances). Everything which happens to it is a consequence of its idea or its being and nothing determines it except God only. It is for this reason that a person of exalted mind and revered saintliness may say that the soul ought often to think as if there were only God and itself in the world. Nothing can make us hold to immortality more firmly than this independence and vastness of the soul which protects it completely against exterior things, since it alone constitutes our universe and together with God is sufficient for itself. It is as impossible for it to perish save through annihilation as it is impossible for the universe to destroy itself, the universe whose animate and perpetual expression it is. Furthermore, the changes in this extended mass which is called our body cannot possibly affect the soul nor can the dissipation of the body destroy that which is indivisible.

XXXIII. Explanation of the relation between the soul and the body, a matter which has been regarded as inexplicable or else as miraculous; concerning the origin of confused perceptions.

We can also see the explanation of that great mystery "the union of the soul and the body," that is to say how it comes about that the passions and actions of the one are accompanied by the actions and passions or else the appropriate phenomena of the other. For it is not possible to conceive how one can have an influence upon the other and it is unreasonable to have recourse at once to the extraordinary intervention of the universal cause in an ordinary and particular case. The following, however, is the true explanation. We have said that everything which happens to a soul or to any substance is a consequence of its concept; hence the idea itself or the essence of the soul brings it about that all of its appearances or perceptions should be born out of its nature and precisely in such a way that they correspond of themselves to that which happens in the universe at large, but more particularly and more perfectly to that which happens in the body associated with it, because it is in a particular way and only for a certain time according to the relation of other bodies to its own body that the soul expresses the state of the universe. This last fact enables us to see how our body belongs to us, without, however, being attached to our essence. I believe that those who are careful thinkers will decide favorably for our principles because of this single reason, viz., that they are able to see in what consists the relation between the soul and the body, a parallelism which appears inexplicable in any other way. We can also see that the perceptions of our senses even when they are clear must necessarily contain certain confused elements, for as all the bodies in the universe are in sympathy, ours receives the impressions of all the others, and while our senses respond to everything, our soul cannot pay attention to every particular. That is why our confused sensations are the result of a variety of perceptions. This variety is infinite. It is almost like the confused murmuring which is heard by those who approach the shore of a sea. It comes from the continual beatings of innumerable waves. If now, out of many perceptions which do not at all fit together to make one, no particular one perception surpasses the others, and if they make impressions about equally strong or equally capable of holding the attention of the soul, they can be perceived only confusedly.

XXXIV. Concerning the difference between spirits and other substances, souls or substantial forms; that the immortality which men desire includes memory.

Supposing that the bodies which constitute a *unum per se*, as human bodies, are substances, and have substantial forms, and supposing that animals have souls, we are obliged to grant that these souls and these substantial forms cannot entirely perish, any more than can the atoms or the ultimate elements of matter, according to the position of other philosophers; for no substance perishes, although it may become very different. Such substances also express the whole universe, although more imperfectly than do spirits. The principal difference, however, is that they do not know that they are, nor what they are. Consequently, not being able to reason, they are unable to discover necessary and universal truths. It is also because they do not reflect regarding themselves that they have no moral qualities, whence it follows that undergoing a thousand transformations, as we see a caterpillar change into a butterfly, the result from a moral or practical standpoint is the same as if we said that they perished in each case, and we can indeed say it from the physical standpoint in the same way that we say bodies perish in their dissolution. But the intelligent soul, knowing that it is and having the ability to say that word "I" so full of meaning, not only continues and exists, metaphysically far more certainly than do the others, but it remains the same from the moral standpoint, and constitutes the same personality, for it is its memory or knowledge of this ego which renders it open to punishment and reward. Also the immortality which is required in morals and in religion does not consist merely in this perpetual existence, which pertains to all substances, for if in addition there were no remembrance of what one had been, immortality would not be at all desirable. Suppose that some individual could suddenly become King of China on condition, however, of forgetting what he had been, as though being born again, would it not amount to the same practically, or as far as the effects could be perceived, as if the individual were annihilated, and a king of China were the same instant created in his place? The individual would have no reason to desire this.

XXXV. The excellence of spirits; that God considers them preferable to other creatures; that the spirits express God rather than the world, while other simple substances express the world rather than God.

In order, however, to prove by natural reasons that God will preserve forever not only our substance, but also our personality, that is to say the recollection and knowledge of what we are (although the distinct knowledge is sometimes suspended during sleep and in swoons) it is necessary to join to metaphysics moral considerations. God must be considered not only as the principle and the cause of all substances and of all existing things, but also as the chief of all persons or intelligent substances, as the absolute monarch of the most perfect city or republic, such as is constituted by all the spirits together in the universe, God being the most complete of all spirits at the same time that he is greatest of all beings. For assuredly the spirits are the most perfect of substances and best express the divinity. Since all the nature, purpose, virtue and function of substances is, as has been sufficiently explained, to express God and the universe, there is no room for doubting that those substances which give the expression, knowing what they are doing and which are able to understand the great truths about God and the universe, do express God and the universe incomparably better than do those natures which are either brutish and incapable of recognizing truths, or are wholly destitute of sensation and knowledge. The difference between intelligent substances and those which are not intelligent is quite as great as between a mirror and one who sees. As God is himself the greatest and wisest of spirits it is easy to understand that the spirits with which he can, so to speak, enter into conversation and even into social relations by communicating to them in particular ways his feelings and his will so that they are able to know and love their benefactor, must be much nearer to him than the rest of created things which may be regarded as the instruments of spirits. In the same way we see that all wise persons consider far more the condition of a man than of anything else however precious it may be; and it seems that the greatest satisfaction which a soul, satisfied in other respects, can have is to see itself loved by others. However, with respect to God there is this difference that his glory and our worship can add nothing to his satisfaction, the recognition of creatures being nothing but a consequence of his sovereign and perfect felicity and being far from contributing to it or from causing it even in part. Nevertheless, that which is reasonable in finite spirits is found eminently in him and as we praise a king who prefers to preserve the life of a man before that of the most precious and rare of his animals, we should not doubt that the most enlightened and most just of all monarchs has the same preference.

XXXVI. God is the monarch of the most perfect republic composed of all the spirits, and the happiness of this city of God is his principal purpose.

Spirits are of all substances the most capable of perfection and their perfections are different in this that they interfere with one another the least, or rather they aid one another the most, for only the most virtuous can be the most perfect friends. Hence it follows that God who in all things has the greatest perfection will have the greatest care for spirits and will give not only to all of them in general, but even to each one in particular the highest perfection which the universal harmony will permit. We can even say that it is because he is a spirit that God is the originator of existences, for if he had lacked the power of will to choose what is best, there would have been no reason why one possible being should exist rather than any other. Therefore God's being a spirit himself dominates all the consideration which he may have toward created things. Spirits alone are made in his image, being as it were of his blood or as children in the family, since they alone are able to serve him of free will, and to act consciously imitating the divine nature. A single spirit is worth a whole world, because it not only expresses the whole world, but it also knows it and governs itself as does God. In this way we may say that though every substance expresses the whole universe, yet the other substances express the world rather than God, while spirits express God rather than the world. This nature of spirits, so noble that it enables them to approach divinity as much as is possible for created things, has as a result that God derives infinitely more glory from them than from the other beings, or rather the other beings furnish to spirits the material for glorifying him. This moral quality of God which constitutes him Lord and Monarch of spirits influences him so to speak personally and in a unique way. It is through this that he humanizes himself, that he is willing to suffer anthropologies, and that he enters into social relations with us and this consideration is so dear to him that the happy and prosperous condition of his empire which consists in the greatest possible felicity of its inhabitants, becomes supreme among his laws. Happiness is to persons what perfection is to beings. And if the dominant principle in the existence of the physical world is the decree to give it the greatest possible perfection, the primary purpose in the moral world or in the city of God which constitutes the noblest part of the universe ought to be to extend the greatest happiness possible. We must not therefore doubt that God has so ordained everything that spirits not only shall live forever, because this is unavoidable, but that they shall also preserve forever their moral quality, so that his city may never lose a person, quite in the same way that the world never loses a substance.

Consequently they will always be conscious of their being, otherwise they would be open to neither reward nor punishment, a condition which is the essence of a republic, and above all of the most perfect republic where nothing can be neglected. In fine, God being at the same time the most just and the most debonnaire of monarchs, and requiring only a good will on the part of men, provided that it be sincere and intentional, his subjects cannot desire a better condition. To render them perfectly happy he desires only that they love him.

XXXVII. Jesus Christ has revealed to men the mystery and the admirable laws of the kingdom of heaven, and the greatness of the supreme happiness which God has prepared for those who love him.

The ancient philosophers knew very little of these important truths. Jesus Christ alone has expressed them divinely well, and in a way so clear and simple that the dullest minds have understood them. His gospel has entirely changed the face of human affairs. It has brought us to know the kingdom of heaven, or that perfect republic of spirits which deserves to be called the city of God. He it is who has discovered to us its wonderful laws. He alone has made us see how much God loves us and with what care everything that concerns us has been provided for; how God, inasmuch as he cares for the sparrows, will not neglect reasoning beings, who are infinitely more dear to him; how all the hairs of our heads are numbered; how heaven and earth may pass away but the word of God and that which belongs to the means of our salvation will not pass away; how God has more regard for the least one among intelligent souls than for the whole machinery of the world; how we ought not to fear those who are able to destroy the body but are unable to destroy the soul, since God alone can render the soul happy or unhappy; and how the souls of the righteous are protected by his hand against all the upheavals of the universe, since God alone is able to act upon them; how none of our acts are forgotten; how everything is to be accounted for; even careless words and even a spoonful of water which is well used; in fact how everything must result in the greatest welfare of the good, for then shall the righteous become like suns and neither our sense nor our minds have ever tasted of anything approaching the joys which God has laid up for those that love him.

The Monadology

1. The monad, of which we will speak here, is nothing else than a simple substance, which goes to make up composites; by simple, we mean without parts.

2. There must be simple substances because there are composites; for a composite is nothing else than a collection or *aggregatum* of simple substances.

3. Now, where there are no constituent parts there is possible neither extension, nor form, nor divisibility. These monads are the true Atoms of nature, and, in fact, the Elements of things.

4. Their dissolution, therefore, is not to be feared and there is no way conceivable by which a simple substance can perish through natural means.

5. For the same reason there is no way conceivable by which a simple substance might, through natural means, come into existence, since it can not be formed by composition.

6. We may say then, that the existence of monads can begin or end only all at once, that is to say, the monad can begin only through creation and end only through annihilation. Composites, however, begin or end gradually.

7. There is also no way of explaining how a monad can be altered or changed in its inner being by any other created thing, since there is no possibility of transposition within it, nor can we conceive of any internal movement which can be produced, directed, increased or diminished there within the substance, such as can take place in the case of composites where a change can occur among the parts. The monads have no windows through which anything may come in or go out. The Attributes are not liable to detach themselves and make an excursion outside the substance, as could *sensible species* of the Schoolmen. In the same way neither substance nor attribute can enter from without into a monad.

8. Still monads must needs have some qualities, otherwise they would not even be existences. And if simple substances did not differ at all in their qualities, there would be no means of perceiving any change in things. Whatever is in a composite can come into it only through its simple elements and the monads, if they were without qualities, since they do not differ at all in quantity, would be indistinguishable one from another. For instance, if we imagine *a plenum* or completely filled space, where each part receives only the equivalent of its own previous motion, one state of things would not be distinguishable from another.

9. Each monad, indeed, must be different from every other. For there are never in nature two beings which are exactly alike, and in which it is not possible to find a difference either internal or based on

an intrinsic property.

10. I assume it as admitted that every created being, and consequently the created monad, is subject to change, and indeed that this change is continuous in each.

11. It follows from what has just been said, that the natural changes of the monad come from an internal principle, because an external cause can have no influence upon its inner being.

12. Now besides this principle of change there must also be in the monad a manifoldness which changes. This manifoldness constitutes, so to speak, the specific nature and the variety of the simple substances.

13. This manifoldness must involve a multiplicity in the unity or in that which is simple. For since every natural change takes place by degrees, there must be something which changes and something which remains unchanged, and consequently there must be in the simple substance a plurality of conditions and relations, even though it has no parts.

14. The passing condition which involves and represents a multiplicity in the unity, or in the simple substance, is nothing else than what is called Perception. This should be carefully distinguished from Apperception or Consciousness, as will appear in what follows. In this matter the Cartesians have fallen into a serious error, in that they treat as nonexistent those perceptions of which we are not conscious. It is this also which has led them to believe that spirits alone are monads and that there are no souls of animals or other Entelechies, and it has led them to make the common confusion between a protracted period of unconsciousness and actual death. They have thus adopted the Scholastic error that souls can exist entirely separated from bodies, and have even confirmed ill-balanced minds in the belief that souls are mortal.

15. The action of the internal principle which brings about the change or the passing from one perception to another may be called Appetition. It is true that the desire (*l'appetit*) is not always able to attain to the whole of the perception which it strives for, but it always attains a portion of it and reaches new perceptions.

16. We, ourselves, experience a multiplicity in a simple substance, when we find that the most trifling thought of which we are conscious involves a variety in the object. Therefore all those who acknowledge that the soul is a simple substance ought to grant this multiplicity in the monad, and Monsieur Bayle should have found no difficulty in it, as he has done in his *Dictionary*, article "Rorarius."

17. It must be confessed, however, that Perception, and that which depends upon it, are inexplicable by mechanical causes, that is to say, by figures and motions. Supposing that there were a machine whose structure produced thought, sensation, and perception, we could conceive of it as increased in size with the same proportions until one

was able to enter into its interior, as he would into a mill. Now, on going into it he would find only pieces working upon one another, but never would he find anything to explain Perception. It is accordingly in the simple substance, and not in the composite nor in a machine that the Perception is to be sought. Furthermore, there is nothing besides perceptions and their changes to be found in the simple substance. And it is in these alone that all the internal activities of the simple substance can consist.

18. All simple substances or created monads may be called Entelechies, because they have in themselves a certain perfection (ἔχουσι τὸ ἐντελές). There is in them a sufficiency (αὐτάρκεια) which makes them the source of their internal activities, and renders them, so to speak, incorporeal Automatons.

19. If we wish to designate as soul everything which has perceptions and desires in the general sense that I have just explained, all simple substances or created monads could be called souls. But since feeling is something more than a mere perception I think that the general name of monad or entelechy should suffice for simple substances which have only perception, while we may reserve the term Soul for those whose perception is more distinct and is accompanied by memory.

20. We experience in ourselves a state where we remember nothing and where we have no distinct perception, as in periods of fainting, or when we are overcome by a profound, dreamless sleep. In such a state the soul does not sensibly differ at all from a simple monad. As this state, however, is not permanent and the soul can recover from it, the soul is something more.

21. Nevertheless it does not follow at all that the simple substance is in such a state without perception. This is so because of the reasons given above; for it cannot perish, nor on the other hand would it exist without some affection and the affection is nothing else than its perception. When, however, there are a great number of weak perceptions where nothing stands out distinctively, we are stunned; as when one turns around and around in the same direction, a dizziness comes on, which makes him swoon and makes him able to distinguish nothing. Among animals, death can occasion this state for quite a period.

22. Every present state of a simple substance is a natural consequence of its preceding state, in such a way that its present is big with its future.

23. Therefore, since on awakening after a period of unconsciousness we become conscious of our perceptions, we must, without having been conscious of them, have had perceptions immediately before; for one perception can come in a natural way only from another perception, just as a motion can come in a natural way

only from a motion.

24. It is evident from this that if we were to have nothing distinctive, or so to speak prominent, and of a higher flavor in our perceptions, we should be in a continual state of stupor. This is the condition of monads which are wholly bare.

25. We see that nature has given to animals heightened perceptions, having provided them with organs which collect numerous rays of light or numerous waves of air and thus make them more effective in their combination. Something similar to this takes place in the case of smell, in that of taste and of touch, and perhaps in many other senses which are unknown to us. I shall have occasion very soon to explain how that which occurs in the soul represents that which goes on in the sense-organs.

26. The memory furnishes a sort of consecutiveness which imitates reason but is to be distinguished from it. We see that animals when they have the perception of something which they notice and of which they have had a similar previous perception, are led by the representation of their memory to expect that which was associated in the preceding perception, and they come to have feelings like those which they had before. For instance, if a stick be shown to a dog, he remembers the pain which it has caused him and he whines or runs away.

27. The vividness of the picture, which comes to him or moves him, is derived either from the magnitude or from the number of the previous perceptions. For, oftentimes, a strong impression brings about, all at once, the same effect as a long-continued habit or as a great many re-iterated, moderate perceptions.

28. Men act in like manner as animals, in so far as the sequence of their perceptions is determined only by the law of memory, resembling the *empirical physicians* who practice simply, without any theory, and we are empiricists in three-fourths of our actions. For instance, when we expect that there will be day-light to-morrow, we do so empirically, because it has always happened so up to the present time. It is only the astronomer who uses his reason in making such an affirmation.

29. But the knowledge of eternal and necessary truths is that which distinguishes us from mere animals and gives us reason and the sciences, thus raising us to a knowledge of ourselves and of God. This is what is called in us the Rational Soul or the Mind.

30. It is also through the knowledge of necessary truths and through abstractions from them that we come to perform Reflective Acts, which cause us to think of what is called the I, and to decide that this or that is within us. It is thus, that in thinking upon ourselves we think of *being*, of *substance*, of the *simple* and *composite*, of a *material* thing and of God himself, conceiving that what is limited in us is in him without limits. These Reflective Acts furnish the principal objects of our reasonings.

31. Our reasoning is based upon two great principles: first, that of Contradiction, by means of which we decide that to be false which involves contradiction and that to be true which contradicts or is opposed to the false.

32. And second, the principle of Sufficient Reason, in virtue of which we believe that no fact can be real or existing and no statement true unless it has a sufficient reason why it should be thus and not otherwise. Most frequently, however, these reasons cannot be known by us.

33. There are also two kinds of Truths: those of Reasoning and those of Fact. The Truths of Reasoning are necessary, and their opposite is impossible. Those of Fact, however, are contingent, and their opposite is possible. When a truth is necessary, the reason can be found by analysis in resolving it into simpler ideas and into simpler truths until we reach those which are primary.

34. It is thus that with mathematicians the Speculative Theorems and the practical Canons are reduced by analysis to Definitions, Axioms, and Postulates.

35. There are finally simple ideas of which no definition can be given. There are also the Axioms and Postulates or, in a word, the primary principles which cannot be proved and, indeed, have no need of proof. These are identical propositions whose opposites involve express contradictions.

36. But there must be also a sufficient reason for contingent truths or truths of fact; that is to say, for the sequence of the things which extend throughout the universe of created beings, where the analysis into more particular reasons can be continued into greater detail without limit because of the immense variety of the things in nature and because of the infinite division of bodies. There is an infinity of figures and of movements, present and past, which enter into the efficient cause of my present writing, and in its final cause there are an infinity of slight tendencies and dispositions of my soul, present and past.

37. And as all this detail again involves other and more detailed contingencies, each of which again has need of a similar analysis in order to find its explanation, no real advance has been made. Therefore, the sufficient or ultimate reason must needs be outside of the sequence or series of these details of contingencies, however infinite they may be.

38. It is thus that the ultimate reason for things must be a necessary substance, in which the detail of the changes shall be present merely potentially, as in the fountain-head, and this substance we call God.

39. Now, since this substance is a sufficient reason for all the above mentioned details, which are linked together throughout, *there is but one God, and this God is sufficient.*

40. We may hold that the supreme substance, which is unique,

universal and necessary with nothing independent outside of it, which is further a pure sequence of possible being, must be incapable of limitation and must contain as much reality as possible.

41. Whence it follows that God is absolutely perfect, perfection being understood as the magnitude of positive reality in the strict sense, when the limitations or the bounds of those things which have them are removed. There where there are no limits, that is to say, in God, perfection is absolutely infinite.

42. It follows also that created things derive their perfections through the influence of God, but their imperfections come from their own natures, which cannot exist without limits. It is in this latter that they are distinguished from God. An example of this original imperfection of created things is to be found in the natural inertia of bodies.

43. It is true, furthermore, that in God is found not only the source of existences, but also that of essences, in so far as they are real. In other words, he is the source of whatever there is real in the possible. This is because the Understanding of God is in the region of eternal truths or of the ideas upon which they depend, and because without him there would be nothing real in the possibilities of things, and not only would nothing be existent, nothing would be even possible.

44. For it must needs be that if there is a reality in essences or in possibilities or indeed in the eternal truths, this reality is based upon something existent and actual, and, consequently, in the existence of the necessary Being in whom essence includes existence or in whom possibility is sufficient to produce actuality.

45. Therefore God alone (or the Necessary Being) has this prerogative that if he be possible he must necessarily exist, and, as nothing is able to prevent the possibility of that which involves no bounds, no negation, and consequently, no contradiction, this alone is sufficient to establish *a priori* his existence. We have, therefore, proved his existence through the reality of eternal truths. But a little while ago we also proved it *a posteriori*, because contingent beings exist which can have their ultimate and sufficient reason only in the necessary being which, in turn, has the reason for existence in itself.

46. Yet we must not think that the eternal truths being dependent upon God are therefore arbitrary and depend upon his will, as Descartes seems to have held, and after him M. Poiret. This is the case only with contingent truths which depend upon fitness or the choice of the greatest good; necessarily truths on the other hand depend solely upon his understanding and are the inner objects of it.

47. God alone is the ultimate unity or the original simple substance, of which all created or derivative monads are the products, and arise, so to speak, through the continual outflashings (fulgurations) of the divinity from moment to moment, limited by the receptivity of

the creature to whom limitation is an essential.

48. In God are present: power, which is the source of everything; knowledge, which contains the details of the ideas; and, finally, will, which changes or produces things in accordance with the principle of the greatest good. To these correspond in the created monad, the subject or basis, the faculty of perception, and the faculty of appetition. In God these attributes are absolutely infinite or perfect, while in the created monads or in the entelechies (*perfectihabies*, as Hermolaus Barbarus translates this word), they are imitations approaching him in proportion to the perfection.

49. A created thing is said to act outwardly in so far as it has perfection, and to be acted upon by another in so far as it is imperfect. Thus action is attributed to the monad in so far as it has distinct perceptions, and passion or passivity is attributed in so far as it has confused perceptions.

50. One created thing is more perfect than another when we find in the first that which gives an *a priori* reason for what occurs in the second. This is why we say that one acts upon the other.

51. In the case of simple substances, the influence which one monad has upon another is only ideal. It can have its effect only through the mediation of God, in so far as in the ideas of God each monad can rightly demand that God, in regulating the others from the beginning of things, should have regarded it also. For since one created monad cannot have a physical influence upon the inner being of another, it is only through the primal regulation that one can have dependence upon another.

52. It is thus that among created things action and passivity are reciprocal. For God, in comparing two simple substances, finds in each one reasons obliging him to adapt the other to it; and consequently what is active in certain respects is passive from another point of view, active in so far as what we distinctly know in it serves to give a reason for what occurs in another, and passive in so far as the reason for what occurs in it is found in what is distinctly known in another.

53. Now as there are an infinity of possible universes in the ideas of God, and but one of them can exist, there must be a sufficient reason for the choice of God which determines him to select one rather than another.

54. And this reason is to be found only in the fitness or in the degree of perfection which these worlds possess, each possible thing having the right to claim existence in proportion to the perfection which it involves.

55. This is the cause for the existence of the greatest good; namely, that the wisdom of God permits him to know it, his goodness causes him to choose it, and his power enables him to produce it.

56. Now this interconnection, relationship, or this adaptation of all

things to each particular one, and of each one to all the rest, brings it about that every simple substance has relations which express all the others and that it is consequently a perpetual living mirror of the universe.

57. And as the same city regarded from different sides appears entirely different, and is, as it were multiplied respectively, so, because of the infinite number of simple substances, there are a similar infinite number of universes which are, nevertheless, only the aspects of a single one as seen from the special point of view of each monad.

58. Through this means has been obtained the greatest possible variety, together with the greatest order that may be; that is to say, through this means has been obtained the greatest possible perfection.

59. This hypothesis, moreover, which I venture to call demonstrated, is the only one which fittingly gives proper prominence to the greatness of God. M. Bayle recognized this when in his *Dictionary* (article "Rorarius") he raised objections to it; indeed, he was inclined to believe that I attributed too much to God, and more than it is possible to attribute to him: But he was unable to bring forward any reason why this universal harmony which causes every substance to express exactly all others through the relation which it has with them is impossible.

60. Besides, in what has just been said can be seen the *a priori* reasons why things cannot be otherwise than they are. It is because God, in ordering the whole, has had regard to every part and in particular to each monad; and since the monad is by its very nature representative, nothing can limit it to represent merely a part of things. It is nevertheless true that this representation is, as regards the details of the whole universe, only a confused representation, and is distinct only as regards a small part of them, that is to say, as regards those things which are nearest or greatest in relation to each monad. If the representation were distinct as to the details of the entire universe, each monad would be a Deity. It is not in the object represented that the monads are limited, but in the modifications of their knowledge of the object. In a confused way they reach out to infinity or to the whole, but are limited and differentiated in the degree of their distinct perceptions.

61. In this respect composites are like simple substances, for all space is filled up; therefore, all matter is connected. And in a plenum or filled space every movement has an effect upon bodies in proportion to this distance, so that not only is every body affected by those which are in contact with it and responds in some way to whatever happens to them, but also by means of them the body responds to those bodies adjoining them, and their intercommunication reaches to any distance whatsoever. Consequently every body responds to all that happens in the universe, so that he who saw all could read in each one what is happening everywhere, and even what has happened and what will

happen. He can discover in the present what is distant both as regards space and as regards time; σύμπνοια πάντα,[11] as Hippocrates said. A soul can, however, read in itself only what is there represented distinctly. It cannot all at once open up all its folds, because they extend to infinity.

62. Thus although each created monad represents the whole universe, it represents more distinctly the body which specially pertains to it and of which it constitutes the entelechy. And as this body expresses all the universe through the interconnection of all matter in the plenum, the soul also represents the whole universe in representing this body, which belongs to it in a particular way.

63. The body belonging to a monad, which is its entelechy or soul, constitutes together with the entelechy what may be called a *living being*, and with a soul what is called an *animal*. Now this body of a living being or of an animal is always organic, because every monad is a mirror of the universe is regulated with perfect order there must needs be order also in what represents it, that is to say in the perceptions of the soul and consequently in the body through which the universe is represented in the soul.

64. Therefore every organic body of a living being is a kind of divine machine or natural automaton, infinitely surpassing all artificial automatons. Because a machine constructed by man's skill is not a machine in each of its parts; for instance, the teeth of a brass wheel have parts or bits which to us are not artificial products and contain nothing in themselves to show the use to which the wheel was destined in the machine. The machines of nature, however, that is to say, living bodies, are still machines in their smallest parts *ad infinitum*. Such is the difference between nature and art, that is to say, between divine art and ours.

65. The author of nature has been able to employ this divine and infinitely marvelous artifice, because each portion of matter is not only, as the ancients recognized, infinitely divisible, but also because it is really divided without end, every part into other parts, each one of which has its own proper motion. Otherwise it would be impossible for each portion of matter to express all the universe.

66. Whence we see that there is a world of created things, of living beings, of animals, of entelechies, of souls, in the minutest particle of matter.

67. Every portion of matter may be conceived as like a garden full of plants and like a pond full of fish. But every branch of a plant, every member of an animal, and every drop of the fluids within it, is also such a garden or such a pond.

---

[11] "All things conspire" is what Leibniz means. See note in Latta's edition.—A. R. C.

68. And although the ground and air which lies between the plants of the garden, and the water which is between the fish in the pond, are not themselves plants or fish, yet they nevertheless contain these, usually so small however as to be imperceptible to us.

69. There is, therefore, nothing uncultivated, or sterile or dead in the universe, no chaos, no confusion, save in appearance; somewhat as a pond would appear at a distance when we could see in it a confused movement, and so to speak, a swarming of the fish, without however discerning the fish themselves.

70. It is evident, then, that every living body has a dominating entelechy, which in animals is the soul. The parts, however, of this living body are full of other living beings, plants and animals, which in turn have each one its entelechy or dominating soul.

71. This does not mean, as some who have misunderstood my thought have imagined, that each soul has a quantity or portion of matter appropriated to it or attached to itself for ever, and that it consequently owns other inferior living beings destined to serve it always; because all bodies are in a state of perpetual flux like rivers, and the parts are continually entering in or passing out.

72. The soul, therefore, changes its body only gradually and by degrees, so that it is never deprived all at once of all its organs. There is frequently a metamorphosis in animals, but never metempsychosis or a transmigration of souls. Neither are there souls wholly separate from bodies, nor bodiless spirits. God alone is without body.

73. This is also why there is never absolute generation or perfect death in the strict sense, consisting in the separation of the soul from the body. What we call generation is development and growth, and what we call death is envelopment and diminution.

74. Philosophers have been much perplexed in accounting for the origin of forms, entelechies, or souls. To-day, however, when it has been learned through careful investigations made in plant, insect and animal life, that the organic bodies of nature are never the product of chaos or putrefaction, but always come from seeds in which there was without doubt some *preformation*, it has been decided that not only is the organic body already present before conception, but also a soul in this body, in a word, the animal itself; and it has been decided that, by means of conception the animal is merely made ready for a great transformation, so as to become an animal of another sort. We can see cases somewhat similar outside of generation when grubs become flies and caterpillars butterflies.

75. These little animals, some of which by conception become large animals, may be called spermatic. Those among them which remain in their species, that is to say, the greater part, are born, multiply, and are destroyed, like the larger animals. There are only a few chosen ones which come out upon a greater stage.

76. This, however, is only half the truth. I believe, therefore, that if the animal never actually commences by natural means, no more does it by natural means come to an end. Not only is there no generation, but also there is no entire destruction or absolute death. These reasonings, carried on *a posteriori* and drawn from experience, accord perfectly with the principles which I have above deduced *a priori*.

77. Therefore we may say that not only the soul (the mirror of the indestructible universe) is indestructible, but also the animal itself is, although its mechanism is frequently destroyed in parts and although it puts off and takes on organic coatings.

78. These principles have furnished me the means of explaining on natural grounds the union, or rather the conformity between the soul and the organic body. The soul follows its own laws, and the body likewise follows its own laws. They are fitted to each other in virtue of the pre-established harmony between all substances, since they are all representations of one and the same universe.

79. Souls act in accordance with the laws of final causes through their desires, ends and means. Bodies act in accordance with the laws of efficient causes or of motion. The two realms, that of efficient causes and that of final causes, are in harmony, each with the other.

80. Descartes saw that souls cannot at all impart force to bodies, because there is always the same quantity of force in matter. Yet he thought that the soul could change the direction of bodies. This was, however, because at that time the law of nature which affirms also that conservation of the same total direction in the motion of matter was not known. If he had known that law, he would have fallen upon my system of pre-established harmony.

81. According to this system bodies act as if (to suppose the impossible) there were no souls at all, and souls act as if there were no bodies, and yet both body and soul act as if the one were influencing the other.

82. Although I find that essentially the same thing is true of all living things and animals, which we have just said (namely, that animals and souls begin from the very commencement of the world and that they no more come to an end than does the world) nevertheless, rational animals have this peculiarity, that their little spermatic animals, as long as they remain such, have only ordinary or sensuous souls, but those of them which are, so to speak, elected, attain by actual conception to human nature, and their sensuous souls are raised to the rank of reason and to the prerogative of spirits.

83. Among the differences that there are between ordinary souls and spirits, some of which I have already instanced, there is also this, that while souls in general are living mirrors or images of the universe of created things, spirits are also images of the Deity himself or of the author of nature. They are capable of knowing the system of the

universe, and of imitating some features of it by means of artificial models, each spirit being like a small divinity in its own sphere.

84. Therefore, spirits are able to enter into a sort of social relationship with God, and with respect to them he is not only what an inventor is to his machine (as in his relation to the other created things), but he is also what a prince is to his subjects, and even what a father is to his children.

85. Whence it is easy to conclude that the totality of all spirits must compose the city of God, that is to say, the most perfect state that is possible under the most perfect monarch.

86. This city of God, this truly universal monarchy, is a moral world within the natural world. It is what is noblest and most divine among the works of God. And in it consists in reality the glory of God, because he would have no glory were not his greatness and goodness known and wondered at by spirits. It is also in relation to this divine city that God properly has goodness. His wisdom and his power are shown everywhere.

87. As we established above that there is a perfect harmony between the two natural realms of efficient and final causes, it will be in place here to point out another harmony which appears between the physical realm of nature and the moral realm of grace, that is to say, between God considered as the architect of the mechanism of the world and God considered as the monarch of the divine city of spirits.

88. This harmony brings it about that things progress of themselves toward grace along natural lines, and that this earth, for example, must be destroyed and restored by natural means at those times when the proper government of spirits demands it, for chastisement in the one case and for a reward in the other.

89. We can say also that God, the Architect, satisfies in all respects God the Law-Giver, that therefore sins will bring their own penalty with them through the order of nature, and because of the very structure of things, mechanical though it is. And in the same way the good actions will attain their rewards in mechanical way through their relation to bodies, although this cannot and ought not always to take place without delay.

90. Finally, under this perfect government, there will be no good action unrewarded and no evil action unpunished; everything must turn out for the well-being of the good; that is to say, of those who are not disaffected in this great state, who, after having done their duty, trust in Providence and who love and imitate, as is meet, the Author of all Good, delighting in the contemplation of his perfections according to the nature of that genuine, pure love which finds pleasure in the happiness of those who are loved. It is for this reason that wise and virtuous persons work in behalf of everything which seems conformable to presumptive or antecedent will of God, and are,

nevertheless, content with what God actually brings to pass through his secret, consequent and determining will, recognizing that if we were able to understand sufficiently well the order of the universe, we should find that it surpasses all the desires of the wisest of us, and that it is impossible to render it better than it is, not only for all in general, but also for each one of us in particular, provided that we have the proper attachment for the author of all, not only as the Architect and the efficient cause of our being, but also as our Lord and the Final Cause, who ought to be the whole goal of our will, and who alone can make us happy.

THE END